MW01443810
COSORI
4-in-1 AIR FRYER
COOKBOOK FOR BEGINNERS
WITH PICTURES
1200 Days of Mind-blowing Recipes to Air fry, Reheat, Roast & Bake your Favorite Gourmet Meals. Including 28-Day Meal Plan
Eva Williams

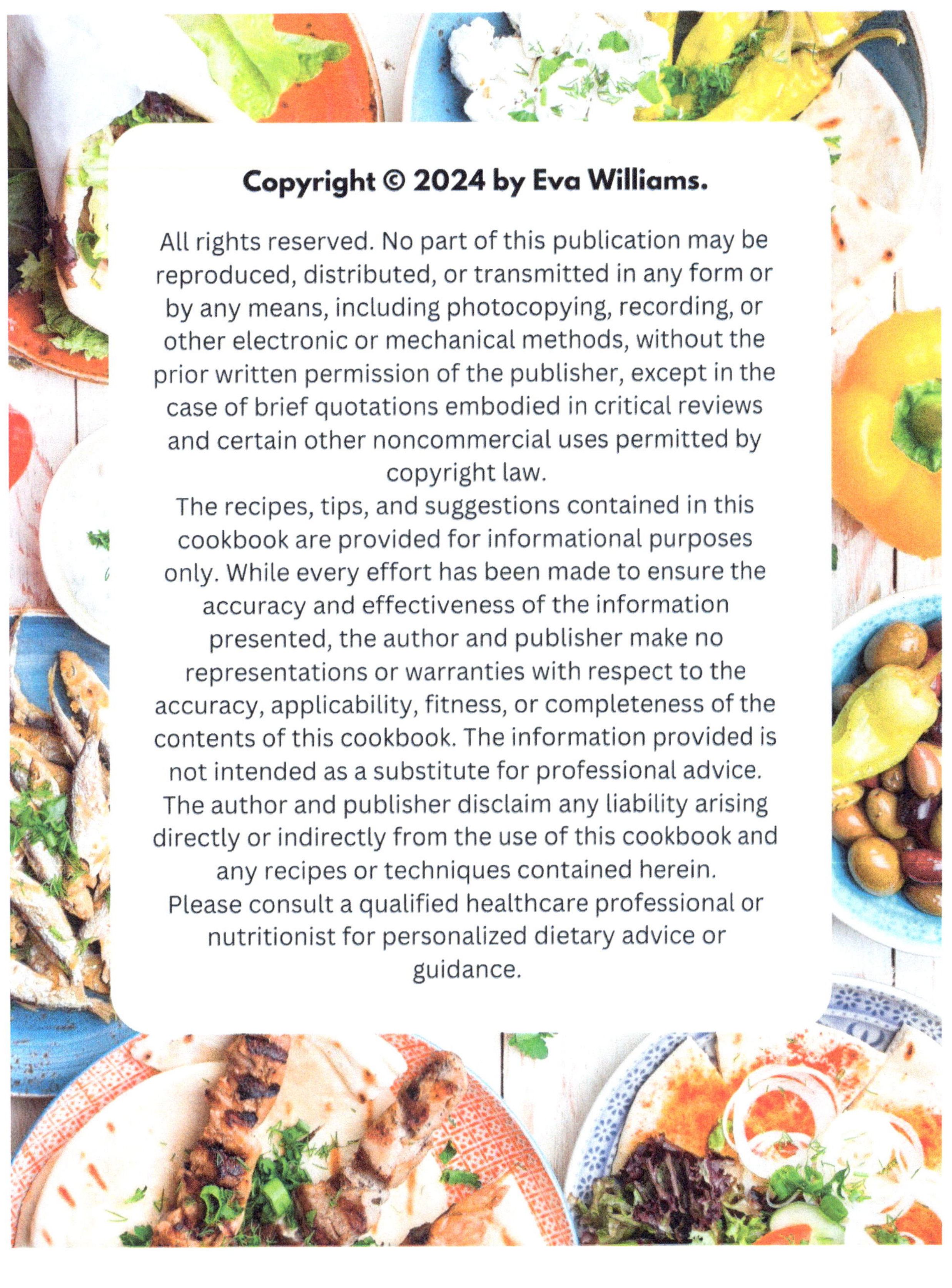

Table of Contents

INTRODUCTION

Welcome to a healthier, quicker, and more convenient way of cooking—air frying! If you're new to air frying, you're about to discover a world where you can enjoy the crispy, golden textures you love without the guilt. Air frying uses up to 97% less oil than traditional frying methods, making it an excellent choice for those who want to indulge in their favorite fried foods while maintaining a balanced diet. Beyond just frying, this versatile appliance can also roast, bake, and reheat, opening up a wide range of culinary possibilities.

Introducing the **Cosori 4-in-1 Air Fryer**, a compact yet powerful kitchen companion designed to make your cooking experience easier and more enjoyable. Whether you're preparing a quick snack, roasting a hearty meal, or reheating leftovers, this air fryer has got you covered. With its 2.1-quart capacity, it's the perfect size for single servings, making it ideal for individuals or small households. Plus, its compact and portable design ensures it fits seamlessly into any kitchen, no matter the size.

The **Air Fry** section will introduce you to the classic crispy textures that have made air fryers a kitchen staple. From golden French fries to crunchy chicken wings, these recipes are designed to satisfy your cravings with a fraction of the oil.

In the **Roast** section, you'll explore hearty dishes perfect for family dinners or cozy nights in. Imagine juicy roasted vegetables, tender meats, and perfectly caramelized flavors—all achieved with minimal effort.

For those with a sweet tooth, the **Bake** section will be a delightful surprise. Yes, your Cosori Air Fryer can bake! From gooey brownies to fluffy muffins, you'll learn how to create bakery-quality treats right in your kitchen.

And let's not forget the **Reheat** section, which will show you how to bring leftovers back to life. Say goodbye to soggy microwaved meals—your air fryer will make your food taste just as fresh as when it was first cooked.

As a special bonus, we've included a **28-Day Meal Plan** at the end of the book. This plan is designed to take the guesswork out of meal planning, offering you a balanced variety of dishes to keep your palate excited and your body nourished. Each week, you'll enjoy a mix of breakfasts, lunches, dinners, and even some snacks, all crafted to fit seamlessly into your busy lifestyle.

In this cookbook, you'll find a carefully curated selection of recipes that showcase the versatility of your Cosori 4-in-1 Air Fryer. From crispy snacks to succulent roasts, each recipe is designed to help you get the most out of your air fryer. We've also included a 28-day meal plan to kickstart your culinary journey, offering a balanced mix of meals that are as delicious as they are easy to prepare. Whether you're a beginner or an experienced cook, this book is your guide to mastering the art of air frying with the Cosori 4-in-1 Air Fryer. Get ready to embark on a 1200-day journey of mouth-watering recipes that will transform the way you cook!

Getting Started with Your Cosori 4-in-1 Air Fryer

Unboxing and First-Time Setup

When you first unbox your Cosori 4-in-1 Air Fryer, you'll notice its sleek and compact design, perfect for any kitchen countertop. The first step is to familiarize yourself with the different components: the main unit, the 2.1-quart cooking basket, and the nonstick crisper plate. Carefully remove all packaging materials, and give the basket and crisper plate a quick wash with warm, soapy water before your first use. Once dry, reassemble your air fryer by placing the crisper plate inside the basket. Now, plug in your air fryer, and you're ready to begin!

Overview of the 2.1-Qt Capacity and What It Means for Cooking

The Cosori 4-in-1 Air Fryer comes with a 2.1-quart capacity, making it an excellent choice for cooking single servings or small portions. This size is ideal for preparing sides, snacks, or meals for one or two people. Despite its compact size, it's capable of delivering powerful cooking performance. You can cook up to a pound of fries or several wings in one go, and its small footprint means it heats up quickly and evenly, ensuring perfect results every time.

Detailed Guide on the 4 Cooking Functions: Air Fry, Roast, Bake, Reheat

Your Cosori 4-in-1 Air Fryer is equipped with four versatile cooking functions:

- **Air Fry**: This function circulates hot air around your food, creating a crispy exterior while keeping the inside tender. It's perfect for making guilt-free versions of your favorite fried foods like fries, chicken wings, and onion rings, with little to no oil.
- **Roast**: The roast function is ideal for cooking meats, vegetables, and other hearty dishes. It provides a steady, high heat that helps caramelize the outside while keeping the inside juicy and flavorful. Use it to prepare dishes like roasted chicken, vegetables, and even small cuts of beef or pork.
- **Bake**: Yes, your air fryer can bake too! This function allows you to make baked goods like muffins, cakes, and cookies with ease. The even heat distribution ensures that your treats come out perfectly baked every time.
- **Reheat**: Say goodbye to soggy leftovers. The reheat function uses gentle, consistent heat to warm up your food while maintaining its original texture. It's perfect for reheating pizza, sandwiches, and other foods that tend to lose their crispiness in the microwave.

Tips for Maintaining and Cleaning Your Air Fryer

To keep your Cosori Air Fryer in top condition, follow these simple maintenance tips:

- **Cleaning**: After each use, make sure to clean the basket and crisper plate. Both are dishwasher-safe, making cleanup a breeze. If you prefer hand washing, use warm, soapy water and a non-abrasive sponge to avoid scratching the nonstick coating. Wipe down the interior and exterior of the air fryer with a damp cloth.
- **Prevention**: Avoid using metal utensils or abrasive cleaners on the nonstick surfaces to prevent damage. Regularly check the air fryer for any signs of wear, and ensure the vent openings are free from obstructions.

- **Storage**: Store your air fryer in a cool, dry place when not in use. If you plan to store it for an extended period, consider placing the unit back in its original box to protect it from dust and damage.

Safety Precautions and Troubleshooting Common Issues

To ensure safe operation of your Cosori Air Fryer, keep these safety tips in mind:

- **Placement**: Always place the air fryer on a stable, heat-resistant surface. Ensure there's adequate space around the appliance for ventilation during use.
- **Overfilling**: Never overfill the basket, as this can affect cooking performance and potentially cause the food to cook unevenly.
- **Handling**: Be cautious when handling the basket after cooking, as it can get very hot. Use oven mitts or tongs to remove food.
- **Power Issues**: If the air fryer isn't turning on, check that it's properly plugged in and the outlet is functioning. If the unit suddenly stops during cooking, it may be due to overheating—unplug it, let it cool down, and then try again.

By following these guidelines, you'll be well on your way to mastering your Cosori 4-in-1 Air Fryer and enjoying delicious, hassle-free meals.

Understanding the Basics of Air Frying

The Science Behind Air Frying: How It Works

Air frying is a modern cooking technique that uses rapidly circulating hot air to cook food. Unlike traditional frying, which submerges food in hot oil, air frying requires little to no oil to achieve similar crispy results. The magic lies in the air fryer's powerful fan and heating element. As the heating element warms the air inside the cooking chamber, the fan circulates this hot air around the food at high speed. This rapid air circulation creates a convection effect, evenly cooking the food from all sides. The result is a crispy, golden exterior and a tender interior—similar to deep-frying but without the excessive use of oil.

The Cosori 4-in-1 Air Fryer, with its compact 2.1-quart capacity, maximizes this technology, allowing for efficient heat distribution even in a smaller space. This ensures that your food is cooked evenly and quickly, making it a convenient option for fast, healthy meals.

Benefits of Air Frying: Healthier Cooking with Up to 97% Less Oil

One of the most significant benefits of air frying is the dramatic reduction in oil usage. Traditional frying methods require food to be submerged in oil, which can significantly increase the calorie and fat content of your meals. With air frying, you can achieve the same crispy texture and delicious flavor using up to 97% less oil. This not only makes your meals healthier but also cuts down on the mess and hassle of dealing with large amounts of hot oil.

In addition to being lower in fat, air-fried foods often retain more nutrients than those cooked using traditional frying methods. The shorter cooking times and lower temperatures help preserve vitamins and minerals that might otherwise be lost. Moreover, air frying produces fewer harmful compounds, such as acrylamide, which can form in starchy foods when cooked at high temperatures using traditional frying methods.

Understanding Temperature and Cooking Times: Tips for Perfect Results

To get the best results from your Cosori 4-in-1 Air Fryer, it's essential to understand the relationship between temperature and cooking time. Here are a few tips to help you master air frying:

- **Preheating**: While the Cosori air fryer heats up quickly, preheating can help achieve more consistent results, especially for recipes that require high temperatures. Preheating ensures that the food starts cooking immediately at the desired temperature, leading to a better texture.
- **Temperature Ranges**: The Cosori 4-in-1 Air Fryer operates between 170°F and 400°F. Lower temperatures are ideal for reheating and dehydrating, while higher temperatures are perfect for achieving that crispy exterior on fried foods. For roasting and baking, moderate temperatures around 300°F to 350°F are typically used.
- **Cooking Times**: Air frying often requires shorter cooking times than traditional methods due to the efficient heat distribution. As a general rule, check your food a few minutes before the recommended cooking time to avoid overcooking. Small, thin pieces of food will cook faster, so adjust times accordingly.
- **Shaking and Turning**: For even cooking, especially with smaller items like fries or vegetables, shake or turn the food halfway through the cooking process. This ensures all sides are exposed to the hot air, resulting in a uniform crispness.

Air Frying Essentials

Best Practices for Air Frying

Tips for Using Less Oil

One of the key benefits of air frying is the ability to cook with significantly less oil while still achieving delicious results. To make the most of this, follow these tips:

- **Use an Oil Sprayer**: Instead of pouring oil directly onto your food, use an oil sprayer to apply a light, even coating. This ensures that just the right amount of oil is used, preventing your food from becoming greasy.
- **Opt for High-Smoke Point Oils**: Oils like avocado oil, grapeseed oil, or olive oil are great choices for air frying. They have high smoke points, which means they won't break down at the high temperatures used in air frying, preserving the flavor and nutritional benefits.
- **Mix Oil with Spices**: If you're using dry rubs or spices, mixing a small amount of oil with the seasoning can help it adhere better to the food, enhancing the flavor and crispiness.

How to Achieve the Perfect Crispiness

Achieving the perfect crispy texture is one of the main goals in air frying. Here's how to get it right every time:

- **Don't Overcrowd the Basket**: Allowing hot air to circulate freely around your food is essential for even cooking. Overcrowding the basket can lead to uneven results and prevent that desired crispiness. Cook in batches if necessary to ensure each piece has enough space.
- **Preheat When Necessary**: While the Cosori air fryer heats up quickly, preheating can help achieve a better crisp, especially for foods that require high temperatures, like fries or chicken wings.
- **Shake or Flip**: Halfway through the cooking process, shake the basket or flip the food to expose all sides to the circulating hot air. This ensures even browning and crispiness.
- **Add a Light Coating of Oil**: A light coating of oil is often enough to create a crispy texture without adding excessive fat. If you're air frying something breaded or coated, a quick spray of oil can help enhance the crispiness.

Cooking Different Types of Food: Frozen, Fresh, and Marinated

Different types of food require slightly different approaches when air frying:

- **Frozen Foods**: Most frozen foods are designed to cook directly from frozen, making them ideal for air frying. Simply place the frozen food in the basket and set the temperature and time according to the package instructions, or slightly reduce the time for even crisper results.
- **Fresh Foods**: For fresh ingredients like vegetables or meat, ensure they are patted dry before cooking. Excess moisture can prevent them from crisping up. Lightly coat with oil and seasoning before air frying for the best flavor and texture.
- **Marinated Foods**: When cooking marinated foods, it's important to let excess marinade drip off before placing the food in the air fryer. This prevents the marinade from burning and ensures the food cooks evenly. Depending on the marinade's sugar content, you may need to lower the temperature slightly to prevent caramelization from happening too quickly.

Essential Tools and Accessories

Recommended Tools for the Best Air Frying Experience

To elevate your air frying experience, consider investing in a few essential tools:

- **Silicone Tongs**: These are perfect for flipping and handling food without scratching the nonstick surface of your air fryer basket.
- **Oil Sprayer**: A refillable oil sprayer allows you to control the amount of oil you use, ensuring an even, light coating on your food.
- **Silicone or Metal Skewers**: Ideal for making kebabs or roasting smaller items like cherry tomatoes or shrimp.
- **Baking Parchment or Liners**: These can help prevent food from sticking to the basket, making cleanup even easier.

Overview of Dishwasher-Safe, Nonstick, BPA-Free Accessories

Your Cosori 4-in-1 Air Fryer comes with a selection of dishwasher-safe, nonstick, and BPA-free accessories, which make both cooking and cleanup a breeze:

- **Nonstick Basket**: The basket is coated with a durable, nonstick surface, ensuring that your food won't stick and making cleanup simple. It's also dishwasher-safe, so you can toss it in after use for easy cleaning.
- **Crisper Plate**: The crisper plate elevates food above the bottom of the basket, allowing air to circulate underneath for even cooking. Like the basket, it's nonstick, BPA-free, and dishwasher-safe.
- **Baking Accessories**: Optional accessories like silicone baking molds or racks can expand your air fryer's capabilities, allowing you to bake cakes, muffins, or even roast multiple items at once.

Tips and Tricks

Maximizing the Potential of Your Cosori Air Fryer

Time-Saving Hacks and Cooking Shortcuts

To make the most of your Cosori 4-in-1 Air Fryer, here are some time-saving hacks and shortcuts that will help you streamline your cooking process:

- **Batch Cooking**: If you're preparing meals for the week, batch cooking is your best friend. Use your air fryer to cook larger quantities of ingredients like chicken breasts, roasted vegetables, or even boiled eggs, then store them in the fridge for easy access throughout the week.
- **Prepping Ingredients Ahead**: Chop, season, and marinate your ingredients ahead of time. Store them in the fridge so that when it's time to cook, you can simply toss them in the air fryer and get your meal on the table in minutes.
- **Use the Reheat Function**: Instead of using the oven or microwave, use the reheat function on your Cosori air fryer for a faster and more effective way to warm up leftovers. This method retains the texture and flavor of your food better than other reheating methods.
- **Frozen to Crispy**: Skip the defrosting step for many frozen foods, and cook them directly in the air fryer. This can save you valuable time and still give you crispy, delicious results.

Customizing Recipes to Your Taste

Your Cosori Air Fryer allows for great flexibility when it comes to tailoring recipes to your specific preferences:

- **Adjust Seasonings**: Don't be afraid to experiment with different seasonings and spice blends to match your taste. Start with small adjustments, then gradually increase to find the perfect balance of flavors.
- **Modify Cooking Times**: Depending on your preferences for crispiness or doneness, you can adjust the cooking times. For example, if you like your fries extra crispy, add a few more minutes to the air frying time.
- **Try Different Oils**: While olive oil is a popular choice, consider experimenting with other oils like coconut, sesame, or avocado to give your dishes unique flavors.

Utilizing the Quiet Operation for Multi-Tasking

One of the standout features of the Cosori 4-in-1 Air Fryer is its quiet operation. With noise levels under 48dB, you can easily multi-task while cooking:

- **Cook While Working or Studying**: The quiet operation allows you to cook without disturbing your work or study environment. Set your air fryer to cook while you finish a task, knowing that it won't be a noisy distraction.
- **Entertain Guests**: If you're hosting a gathering, you can continue cooking without interrupting the flow of conversation. The quiet air fryer won't overpower the background noise, allowing you to socialize freely.
- **Early Morning or Late-Night Cooking**: Use the quiet operation to your advantage if you need to cook early in the morning or late at night without waking up others in the household.

Cleaning and Maintenance

Best Practices for Keeping Your Air Fryer in Top Condition

To ensure your Cosori Air Fryer remains in excellent working order, follow these best practices for cleaning and maintenance:

- **Clean After Every Use**: Make it a habit to clean the basket and crisper plate after each use. This prevents food residue from building up, which could affect the performance of your air fryer and alter the taste of your food.
- **Use Warm, Soapy Water**: For hand washing, use warm, soapy water and a non-abrasive sponge to clean the nonstick surfaces. Avoid using harsh chemicals or scouring pads that could damage the coating.
- **Wipe Down the Exterior**: Keep the exterior of the air fryer clean by wiping it down regularly with a damp cloth. This removes any fingerprints, splatters, or dust, keeping it looking brand new.
- **Check the Heating Element**: Periodically inspect the heating element for any food particles or grease. If needed, gently wipe it with a damp cloth (ensure the unit is unplugged and cool before doing so).

How to Prolong the Life of Your Air Fryer

Extend the life of your Cosori Air Fryer by following these simple tips:

- **Avoid Overloading**: Don't overload the basket with too much food, as this can strain the air fryer and lead to uneven cooking. Stick to the recommended capacity for optimal results.
- **Handle with Care**: Be gentle when removing and inserting the basket and crisper plate. Avoid dropping or banging the components to prevent any damage.
- **Store Properly**: When not in use, store your air fryer in a cool, dry place. If you're storing it for an extended period, cover it to protect it from dust and potential damage.
- **Follow Manufacturer Guidelines**: Always refer to the user manual for specific care instructions, and follow any recommended maintenance schedules to keep your air fryer running smoothly.

By applying these tips and tricks, you'll not only enhance your cooking experience but also ensure that your Cosori 4-in-1 Air Fryer remains a reliable kitchen companion for years to come.

AIRFRYER BREAKFAST DELIGHTS

Quinoa Breakfast Bowls with Poached Egg and Avocado

Start your day with a nutritious and protein-packed breakfast bowl. This recipe combines fluffy quinoa, a perfectly poached egg, and creamy avocado, creating a delicious and satisfying meal that's ready in minutes.

Tools needed:

Air fryer
Small oven-safe bowl or ramekin
Cooking spray
Pot for boiling quinoa
Knife and cutting board
Fork or spoon for mashing avocado

Ingredients:

- 1/2 cup cooked quinoa
- 1 large egg
- 1/2 ripe avocado, sliced or mashed
- 1/4 cup cherry tomatoes, halved
- 1 tbsp extra virgin olive oil
- Salt and pepper to taste
- Fresh herbs (optional, such as parsley, cilantro, or chives)

Directions:

1. **Cook the Quinoa:** Begin by cooking the quinoa. Rinse 1/4 cup of quinoa under cold water, then combine it with 1/2 cup of water in a small pot. Bring to a boil, reduce heat, and simmer for 12-15 minutes or until the water is absorbed and the quinoa is tender. Fluff with a fork and set aside.
2. **Preheat the Air Fryer:** Preheat your air fryer to 350°F (175°C). While it preheats, spray a small oven-safe bowl or ramekin with cooking spray.
3. **Poach the Egg:** Crack the egg into the prepared bowl. Place the bowl in the air fryer basket and cook for 4-6 minutes, depending on how runny or set you prefer the yolk. The whites should be fully cooked, and the yolk should remain soft and runny.
4. **Prepare the Avocado:** While the egg cooks, slice or mash the avocado. If mashing, you can add a pinch of salt and a squeeze of lemon juice to enhance the flavor.
5. **Assemble the Bowl:** In a serving bowl, layer the cooked quinoa as the base. Top with the poached egg, avocado slices or mash, and halved cherry tomatoes.
6. **Season and Garnish:** Drizzle with olive oil, and season with salt and pepper to taste. If desired, garnish with fresh herbs for added flavor and color.

Servings: 1 | **Prep time:** 10 minutes | **Cooking time:** 15 minutes

Nutritional info: Calories: 350, Protein: 12g, Carbs: 28g, Fat: 20g

Quick tips:

- **Adjust Cooking Time for Eggs:** If you prefer a firmer yolk, increase the cooking time by 1-2 minutes.
- **Enhance the Flavor:** For extra flavor, try adding a sprinkle of feta cheese or a dollop of hummus on top of the bowl.
- **Meal Prep:** Cook a larger batch of quinoa ahead of time and store it in the refrigerator for up to 5 days. This will save time in the morning.

Miso-Glazed Sweet Potato Toasts with Avocado

This dish puts a savory twist on traditional avocado toast by replacing the bread with sweet potato slices and adding a rich miso glaze. The combination of sweet and umami flavors, paired with creamy avocado, makes for a delicious and unique breakfast or snack.

Tools needed:

Air fryer
Sharp knife and cutting board
Small mixing bowl
Pastry brush
Fork for mashing avocado

Ingredients:

- 1 large sweet potato, washed and sliced lengthwise into 1/4-inch thick slices
- 1 tbsp white miso paste
- 1 tbsp maple syrup
- 1/2 ripe avocado, mashed or sliced
- 1 tsp sesame seeds (optional, for garnish)
- Salt and pepper to taste

Directions:

1. **Prepare the Sweet Potatoes:** Preheat the air fryer to 375°F (190°C). Carefully slice the sweet potato lengthwise into 1/4-inch thick slices. These slices will serve as your “toast” base.
2. **Air Fry the Sweet Potatoes:** Place the sweet potato slices in a single layer in the air fryer basket. Cook for 10-12 minutes, flipping halfway through, until the slices are tender and slightly crispy on the edges.
3. **Make the Miso Glaze:** While the sweet potatoes are cooking, mix the miso paste and maple syrup in a small bowl until smooth. Adjust the consistency with a few drops of water if needed to create a spreadable glaze.
4. **Glaze the Sweet Potatoes:** Once the sweet potato slices are cooked, remove them from the air fryer. Using a pastry brush, apply a thin layer of the miso glaze to each slice while they are still warm.
5. **Top with Avocado:** Spread the mashed avocado evenly over the glazed sweet potato slices. If using sliced avocado, arrange the slices neatly on top.
6. **Garnish and Season:** Sprinkle the avocado-topped toasts with sesame seeds for added texture. Season with salt and pepper to taste.
7. **Serve:** Serve the sweet potato toasts immediately, while they are still warm and crispy.

Servings: 2
Prep time: 10 minutes
Cooking time: 12 minutes

Nutritional info: Calories: 280, Protein: 4g, Carbs: 35g, Fat: 13g

Quick tips:

- **Even Slicing:** For the best results, slice the sweet potato as evenly as possible. A mandoline slicer can help achieve uniform slices.
- **Customization:** For a spicy kick, add a drizzle of sriracha or sprinkle red pepper flakes on top of the avocado.
- **Meal Prep:** You can cook a batch of sweet potato toasts ahead of time and reheat them in the air fryer for a quick snack or breakfast.

Savory Chia Seed Pancakes with Smoked Salmon

These savory chia seed pancakes are a delightful alternative to traditional sweet pancakes, offering a nutritious base topped with rich smoked salmon. Perfect for a special breakfast or brunch, these pancakes are packed with omega-3s, fiber, and protein.

Tools needed:

Air fryer
Mixing bowl
Whisk or fork
Spatula
Nonstick spray
Small oven-safe dish or baking pan for air fryer

Ingredients:

- 1/2 cup whole wheat flour
- 1 tbsp chia seeds
- 1/4 tsp baking powder
- 1/4 tsp salt
- 1 large egg
- 1/2 cup milk (dairy or non-dairy)
- 1 tbsp olive oil
- 2 oz smoked salmon
- Fresh dill (optional for garnish)
- Lemon wedges (optional for serving)

Directions:

1. **Prepare the Pancake Batter:** In a mixing bowl, combine the whole wheat flour, chia seeds, baking powder, and salt. In a separate bowl, whisk together the egg, milk, and olive oil. Pour the wet ingredients into the dry ingredients and stir until just combined, being careful not to overmix.
2. **Preheat the Air Fryer:** Preheat your air fryer to 350°F (175°C). Lightly spray a small oven-safe dish or pan with nonstick spray.
3. **Cook the Pancakes:** Pour a small amount of batter into the prepared dish, forming pancakes about 3-4 inches in diameter. Place the dish in the air fryer and cook for 5-7 minutes, or until the pancakes are golden brown and cooked through. You may need to cook in batches depending on the size of your dish.
4. **Assemble the Pancakes:** Once the pancakes are cooked, remove them from the air fryer and allow them to cool slightly. Top each pancake with a slice of smoked salmon.
5. **Garnish and Serve:** Garnish with fresh dill and serve with lemon wedges on the side for a burst of freshness.
6. **Serve immediately:** Serve the pancakes warm, with the smoked salmon slightly warmed by the heat of the pancakes.

Servings: 2
Prep time: 10 minutes
Cooking time: 7 minutes per batch

Nutritional info:
Calories: 250
Protein: 12g
Carbs: 20g
Fat: 13g

Quick tips:

- **Make It Gluten-Free:** Substitute the whole wheat flour with a gluten-free flour blend if needed.
- **Enhance the Flavor:** Add finely chopped scallions or chives to the pancake batter for an extra burst of flavor.
- **Perfect Pancake Size:** Use a measuring cup or ladle to pour the batter into the pan to ensure evenly sized pancakes.

Air Fryer Green Shakshuka

Green Shakshuka is a vibrant and nutritious twist on the traditional shakshuka, made with a mix of green vegetables, herbs, and poached eggs. This Middle Eastern-inspired dish is perfect for a hearty breakfast or brunch.

Tools needed:

Air fryer
Medium oven-safe skillet or baking dish
Knife and cutting board
Mixing spoon or spatula

Ingredients:

- 1 tbsp olive oil
- 1 small onion, finely chopped
- 2 cloves garlic, minced
- 1 green bell pepper, chopped
- 2 cups spinach, chopped
- 1/2 cup fresh cilantro, chopped
- 1/2 cup fresh parsley, chopped
- 1/4 cup crumbled feta cheese
- 4 large eggs
- 1/4 tsp ground cumin
- Salt and pepper to taste
- Red pepper flakes (optional, for garnish)

Directions:

1. **Preheat the Air Fryer:** Preheat your air fryer to 350°F (175°C). While preheating, prepare the ingredients.
2. **Cook the Vegetables:** Heat the olive oil in an oven-safe skillet or baking dish over medium heat. Add the chopped onion and garlic, sautéing until soft and fragrant, about 3-4 minutes.
3. **Add the Greens:** Stir in the green bell pepper, spinach, cilantro, and parsley. Cook until the spinach is wilted and the bell pepper is tender, about 5 minutes. Season with cumin, salt, and pepper.
4. **Make Wells for the Eggs:** Use a spoon to create four small wells in the vegetable mixture. Crack an egg into each well, being careful not to break the yolk.
5. **Air Fry the Shakshuka:** Place the skillet or dish into the air fryer basket. Cook at 350°F for 8-10 minutes, or until the egg whites are set but the yolks are still runny.
6. **Finish and Serve:** Remove from the air fryer and sprinkle with crumbled feta cheese. Garnish with red pepper flakes if desired.
7. **Serve immediately:** Serve directly from the skillet with crusty bread for dipping.

Servings: 2
Prep time: 10 minutes
Cooking time: 15 minutes

Nutritional info:
Calories: 300
Protein: 15g
Carbs: 12g
Fat: 22g

Quick tips:

- **Adjust Cooking Time:** For firmer yolks, increase the cooking time by 1-2 minutes.
- **Customize Your Greens:** Substitute or add other green vegetables like kale, Swiss chard, or zucchini.
- **Serve with Bread:** Pair with warm pita or crusty bread to soak up the flavorful sauce.

Zaatar-Spiced Breakfast Flatbreads

These Zaatar-Spiced Breakfast Flatbreads bring Middle Eastern flavors to your morning routine. Topped with a fragrant zaatar blend and fresh toppings, they are perfect for a quick and flavorful breakfast.

Tools needed:

Air fryer
Rolling pin
Baking sheet or air fryer rack
Knife and cutting board

Ingredients:

- 1 cup whole wheat flour
- 1/2 tsp salt
- 1/2 cup warm water
- 1 tbsp olive oil
- 2 tbsp zaatar spice blend
- 1/2 cup plain Greek yogurt
- 1/2 cucumber, thinly sliced
- 1/2 small red onion, thinly sliced
- 1/4 cup cherry tomatoes, halved
- Fresh mint leaves for garnish

Directions:

1. **Prepare the Dough:** In a mixing bowl, combine the whole wheat flour and salt. Gradually add the warm water and olive oil, mixing until a soft dough forms. Knead the dough for 2-3 minutes until smooth. Cover with a damp cloth and let it rest for 10 minutes.
2. **Preheat the Air Fryer:** Preheat your air fryer to 375°F (190°C).
3. **Roll Out the Dough:** Divide the dough into two equal portions. On a lightly floured surface, roll each portion into a flatbread shape, about 1/4-inch thick.
4. **Season with Zaatar:** Place the flatbreads on a baking sheet or air fryer rack. Sprinkle each flatbread with 1 tablespoon of zaatar spice blend, pressing it lightly into the dough.
5. **Air Fry the Flatbreads:** Transfer the flatbreads to the air fryer basket. Cook at 375°F for 8-10 minutes, or until the flatbreads are golden and slightly crispy.
6. **Top the Flatbreads:** Remove the flatbreads from the air fryer and let them cool slightly. Spread a layer of Greek yogurt over each flatbread. Top with cucumber slices, red onion, cherry tomatoes, and fresh mint leaves.
7. **Serve immediately:** Serve the flatbreads warm or at room temperature.

Servings: 2
Prep time: 15 minutes
Cooking time: 10 minutes

Nutritional info:
Calories: 320
Protein: 10g
Carbs: 45g
Fat: 12g

Quick tips:

- **Make Ahead:** Prepare the dough and roll out the flatbreads in advance. Store them in the fridge or freezer until ready to cook.
- **Add Protein:** For a more filling meal, add sliced boiled eggs or crumbled feta on top.
- **Zaatar Substitute:** If you don't have zaatar, you can make your own blend using thyme, sesame seeds, sumac, and a pinch of salt.

Matcha and Coconut Breakfast Bars

These Matcha and Coconut Breakfast Bars are a healthy and energizing start to your day. Made with oats, matcha powder, and coconut, they are packed with antioxidants and fiber, perfect for a grab-and-go breakfast.

Tools needed:

Air fryer
Mixing bowl
Baking dish or pan that fits in the air fryer
Parchment paper

Ingredients:

- 1 cup rolled oats
- 1/4 cup shredded coconut
- 2 tbsp matcha powder
- 1/4 cup honey or maple syrup
- 1/4 cup coconut oil, melted
- 1/4 cup almond butter
- 1/2 tsp vanilla extract
- Pinch of salt

Directions:

1. **Prepare the Air Fryer:** Preheat your air fryer to 320°F (160°C). Line a baking dish or pan with parchment paper, making sure the paper extends over the sides for easy removal.
2. **Mix the Dry Ingredients:** In a large mixing bowl, combine the rolled oats, shredded coconut, matcha powder, and a pinch of salt. Stir until well mixed.
3. **Add the Wet Ingredients:** In a separate bowl, whisk together the honey (or maple syrup), melted coconut oil, almond butter, and vanilla extract until smooth. Pour the wet ingredients into the dry ingredients, mixing until everything is evenly coated.
4. **Form the Bars:** Transfer the mixture to the prepared baking dish. Press the mixture down firmly and evenly with the back of a spoon or spatula.
5. **Air Fry the Bars:** Place the dish in the air fryer basket. Cook at 320°F for 12-15 minutes, or until the edges are golden brown and the bars are set.
6. **Cool and Slice:** Remove the baking dish from the air fryer and let it cool completely. Once cooled, lift the bars out using the parchment paper and cut them into squares or rectangles.
7. **Serve:** Enjoy the bars as a quick breakfast or snack.

Servings: 8 bars
Prep time: 10 minutes
Cooking time: 15 minutes

Nutritional info:
Calories: 180 per bar
Protein: 3g
Carbs: 22g
Fat: 9g

Quick tips:

- **Storage:** Store the bars in an airtight container at room temperature for up to a week or in the refrigerator for longer freshness.
- **Add-ins:** Customize the bars by adding nuts, seeds, or dried fruits to the mixture.
- **Matcha Quality:** Use high-quality matcha powder for the best flavor and nutritional benefits.

Beetroot and Goat Cheese Breakfast Tart

This Beetroot and Goat Cheese Breakfast Tart is a visually stunning and delicious dish that combines the earthy sweetness of roasted beets with the tangy creaminess of goat cheese. It's perfect for a special breakfast or brunch.

Tools needed:

Air fryer
Rolling pin
Baking dish or tart pan that fits in the air fryer
Parchment paper
Knife and cutting board

Ingredients:

- 1 sheet puff pastry, thawed
- 2 medium beetroots, peeled and thinly sliced
- 3 oz goat cheese, crumbled
- 1 tbsp olive oil
- 1 tbsp balsamic vinegar
- 1 tsp fresh thyme leaves
- 1 egg, beaten (for egg wash)
- Salt and pepper to taste

Directions:

1. **Preheat the Air Fryer:** Preheat your air fryer to 350°F (175°C). While it preheats, prepare the ingredients.
2. **Prepare the Puff Pastry:** On a lightly floured surface, roll out the puff pastry sheet to fit your baking dish or tart pan. Line the dish or pan with the puff pastry, trimming any excess. Prick the base with a fork to prevent it from puffing up too much during baking.
3. **Roast the Beetroots:** In a bowl, toss the beetroot slices with olive oil, balsamic vinegar, salt, and pepper. Arrange the slices in a single layer on a baking sheet or dish that fits in your air fryer. Roast in the air fryer for 10-12 minutes until tender and slightly caramelized.
4. **Assemble the Tart:** Spread the crumbled goat cheese evenly over the base of the puff pastry. Arrange the roasted beetroot slices on top of the cheese. Sprinkle with fresh thyme leaves.
5. **Brush with Egg Wash:** Lightly brush the edges of the puff pastry with the beaten egg to give it a golden finish during baking.
6. **Air Fry the Tart:** Place the tart in the air fryer and cook at 350°F for 12-15 minutes, or until the pastry is golden brown and crispy.
7. **Serve:** Remove the tart from the air fryer and let it cool slightly before slicing. Serve warm.

Servings: 4
Prep time: 15 minutes
Cooking time: 25 minutes

Nutritional info:
Calories: 280
Protein: 7g
Carbs: 22g
Fat: 18g

Quick tips:

- **Pre-cook the Beets:** If you're short on time, pre-cook the beets in advance and store them in the fridge until ready to assemble the tart.
- **Add Nuts:** For added crunch, sprinkle some toasted walnuts or pine nuts on top before serving.
- **Serve with Salad:** Pair the tart with a fresh green salad for a balanced breakfast or brunch.

Air Fryer Chickpea Flour Omelette

This Air Fryer Chickpea Flour Omelette is a delicious, protein-packed, and vegan-friendly alternative to traditional omelets. Made with chickpea flour, it's naturally gluten-free and customizable with your favorite veggies and spices.

Tools needed:

Air fryer
Mixing bowl
Whisk or fork
Nonstick spray
Oven-safe dish or pan that fits in the air fryer

Ingredients:

- 1/2 cup chickpea flour (also known as besan or gram flour)
- 1/2 cup water
- 1/4 tsp turmeric powder
- 1/4 tsp cumin powder
- 1/4 tsp baking powder
- Salt and pepper to taste
- 1/4 cup chopped spinach
- 1/4 cup diced tomatoes
- 1/4 cup chopped onions
- 1 tbsp chopped fresh cilantro

Directions:

1. **Preheat the Air Fryer:** Preheat your air fryer to 350°F (175°C).
2. **Prepare the Omelette Batter:** In a mixing bowl, whisk together the chickpea flour, water, turmeric, cumin, baking powder, salt, and pepper until smooth and free of lumps. The batter should have a similar consistency to pancake batter.
3. **Add the Vegetables:** Fold in the chopped spinach, diced tomatoes, onions, and fresh cilantro into the batter.
4. **Prepare the Dish:** Lightly spray an oven-safe dish or pan with nonstick spray. Pour the omelette batter into the dish, spreading it evenly.
5. **Cook the Omelette:** Place the dish in the air fryer basket and cook at 350°F for 12-15 minutes, or until the omelette is set and slightly golden on top.
6. **Serve:** Remove the dish from the air fryer and let the omelette cool for a minute before slicing. Serve warm with your favorite chutney or hot sauce.

Servings: 2
Prep time: 10 minutes
Cooking time: 15 minutes

Nutritional info:
Calories: 180
Protein: 7g
Carbs: 20g
Fat: 6g

Quick tips:

- **Customize the Filling:** Add any vegetables you like, such as bell peppers, mushrooms, or zucchini.
- **Crispy Texture:** For a crispy finish, increase the cooking time by a couple of minutes.
- **Meal Prep:** The batter can be made ahead and stored in the refrigerator for up to 2 days.

Turmeric-Spiced Breakfast Hash with Cauliflower and Carrots

This Turmeric-Spiced Breakfast Hash is a flavorful and healthy dish that's perfect for a morning boost. Packed with vegetables like cauliflower and carrots, and seasoned with warming spices, it's a hearty and nutritious start to the day.

Tools needed:

Air fryer
Large mixing bowl
Knife and cutting board
Spatula

Ingredients:

- 1/2 head of cauliflower, cut into small florets
- 2 medium carrots, peeled and diced
- 1 small onion, finely chopped
- 2 cloves garlic, minced
- 1 tbsp olive oil
- 1 tsp ground turmeric
- 1/2 tsp ground cumin
- 1/2 tsp smoked paprika
- Salt and pepper to taste
- Fresh cilantro (optional for garnish)

Directions:

1. **Preheat the Air Fryer:** Preheat your air fryer to 375°F (190°C).
2. **Prepare the Vegetables:** In a large mixing bowl, combine the cauliflower florets, diced carrots, chopped onion, and minced garlic.
3. **Season the Vegetables:** Drizzle the olive oil over the vegetables and sprinkle with turmeric, cumin, smoked paprika, salt, and pepper. Toss everything together until the vegetables are evenly coated with the spices.
4. **Cook the Hash:** Spread the vegetable mixture in a single layer in the air fryer basket. Cook at 375°F for 15-18 minutes, shaking the basket halfway through cooking, until the vegetables are tender and slightly crispy on the edges.
5. **Serve:** Remove the hash from the air fryer and transfer to a serving plate. Garnish with fresh cilantro if desired and serve warm.

Servings: 2
Prep time: 10 minutes
Cooking time: 18 minutes

Nutritional info:
Calories: 150
Protein: 3g
Carbs: 15g
Fat: 8g

Quick tips:

- **Add Protein:** Top the hash with a poached egg or crispy chickpeas for added protein.
- **Make It Spicy:** For a spicier version, add a pinch of cayenne pepper or red chili flakes to the seasoning mix.
- **Batch Cooking:** Double the recipe and store leftovers in the fridge for up to 3 days; reheat in the air fryer for a quick breakfast.

Air Fryer Quiche with Wild Mushrooms and Gruyere

This Air Fryer Quiche with Wild Mushrooms and Gruyere is a rich and savory dish that combines the earthy flavors of wild mushrooms with the creamy, nutty taste of Gruyere cheese.

Tools needed:

Air fryer
Mixing bowl
Whisk or fork
Rolling pin
6-inch pie dish or tart pan that fits in the air fryer
Knife and cutting board
Skillet for sautéing mushrooms

Ingredients:

- 1 pre-made pie crust (store-bought or homemade)
- 1 cup wild mushrooms, cleaned and sliced
- 1 tbsp olive oil
- 1 small shallot, finely chopped
- 1/2 cup Gruyere cheese, grated
- 3 large eggs
- 1/2 cup heavy cream or whole milk
- 1/4 tsp ground nutmeg
- Salt and pepper to taste
- Fresh thyme leaves (optional, for garnish)

Directions:

Prepare the Pie Crust: Roll out the pie crust on a lightly floured surface to fit your 6-inch pie dish or tart pan. Line the dish with the crust, pressing it gently into the sides and trimming any excess. Prick the bottom of the crust with a fork to prevent it from puffing up during baking.
Pre-cook the Crust: Preheat your air fryer to 350°F (175°C). Place the pie dish in the air fryer and bake the crust for 5-7 minutes until it's lightly golden. Remove from the air fryer and set aside.
Sauté the Mushrooms: While the crust is baking, heat olive oil in a skillet over medium heat. Add the shallots and cook until softened, about 2 minutes. Add the sliced mushrooms and sauté until they are tender and any released moisture has evaporated, about 5-7 minutes. Season with salt and pepper, then remove from heat.
Prepare the Filling: In a mixing bowl, whisk together the eggs, heavy cream, Gruyere cheese, nutmeg, salt, and pepper until well combined.
Assemble the Quiche: Spread the sautéed mushrooms evenly over the pre-cooked pie crust. Pour the egg mixture over the mushrooms, making sure it spreads evenly.
Air Fry the Quiche: Place the quiche in the air fryer and cook at 350°F for 15-18 minutes, or until the filling is set and the top is golden brown. The center should be just slightly jiggly when you shake the dish gently.
Cool and Serve: Remove the quiche from the air fryer and let it cool for a few minutes before slicing. Garnish with fresh thyme leaves if desired.
Serve warm or at room temperature.

Servings: 4 | **Prep time:** 15 minutes | **Cooking time:** 25 minutes
Nutritional info: Calories: 300, Protein: 10g, Carbs: 20g, Fat: 21g

Quick tips:

- **Blind Baking:** If you prefer a crisper crust, consider blind baking the crust with pie weights for the first few minutes before adding the filling.
- **Variety of Mushrooms:** Feel free to use a mix of wild mushrooms like shiitake, cremini, or oyster for a more complex flavor profile.
- **Make It Ahead:** This quiche can be made ahead of time and stored in the refrigerator for up to 2 days.

AIRFRYER POULTRY PERFECTION

Duck Breast with Pomegranate Glaze

This Air Fryer Duck Breast with Pomegranate Glaze is a luxurious dish that's perfect for special occasions or when you want to treat yourself to something extraordinary. The rich, tender duck breast is complemented by a sweet and tangy pomegranate glaze, creating a delightful contrast of flavors.

Tools needed:

Air fryer
Small saucepan
Knife and cutting board
Tongs
Meat thermometer

Ingredients:

- 2 duck breasts, skin on
- 1/2 cup pomegranate juice
- 2 tbsp honey
- 1 tbsp balsamic vinegar
- 1 tsp fresh thyme leaves
- Salt and pepper to taste

Directions:

1. **Prepare the Duck Breasts:** Pat the duck breasts dry with paper towels. Score the skin in a crosshatch pattern, being careful not to cut into the meat. Season both sides generously with salt and pepper.
2. **Preheat the Air Fryer:** Preheat your air fryer to 400°F (200°C).
3. **Cook the Duck Breasts:** Place the duck breasts skin side down in the air fryer basket. Cook at 400°F for 8-10 minutes, then flip and cook for an additional 5-7 minutes, or until the internal temperature reaches 135°F (57°C) for medium-rare. Adjust cooking time based on your preferred level of doneness.
4. **Make the Pomegranate Glaze:** While the duck is cooking, combine pomegranate juice, honey, balsamic vinegar, and fresh thyme in a small saucepan. Bring to a simmer over medium heat, stirring occasionally, until the mixture reduces by half and thickens into a glaze, about 10-12 minutes.
5. **Rest the Duck:** Once the duck breasts are cooked, remove them from the air fryer and let them rest for 5 minutes.
6. **Slice and Glaze:** Slice the duck breasts thinly and drizzle with the pomegranate glaze.
7. **Serve immediately:** Serve warm, garnished with additional fresh thyme if desired.

Servings: 2
Prep time: 10 minutes
Cooking time: 20 minutes

Nutritional info: Calories: 450, Protein: 24g, Carbs: 15g, Fat: 32g

Quick tips:

- **Render the Fat:** For an extra crispy skin, start cooking the duck breasts skin side down in a cold air fryer basket, allowing the fat to render slowly as it heats up.
- **Resting Time:** Letting the duck rest after cooking ensures that the juices redistribute, making the meat more tender.
- **Side Suggestions:** Serve with roasted vegetables or a fresh arugula salad to balance the richness of the duck.

Saffron and Yogurt Marinated Chicken Thighs

These Saffron and Yogurt Marinated Chicken Thighs are infused with the warm, floral notes of saffron and the tangy richness of yogurt, creating a dish that's both flavorful and tender. The air fryer crisps up the exterior while keeping the meat juicy.

Tools needed:

Air fryer
Mixing bowl
Whisk or fork
Knife and cutting board
Plastic wrap or airtight container for marinating

Ingredients:

- 4 boneless, skinless chicken thighs
- 1/2 cup plain Greek yogurt
- 1/4 tsp saffron threads
- 2 tbsp warm water
- 1 tbsp lemon juice
- 2 cloves garlic, minced
- 1 tsp ground cumin
- 1 tsp ground coriander
- Salt and pepper to taste
- Fresh cilantro for garnish (optional)

Directions:

1. **Bloom the Saffron:** In a small bowl, combine the saffron threads with the warm water. Let it steep for 5-10 minutes to release the color and flavor.
2. **Prepare the Marinade:** In a mixing bowl, whisk together the yogurt, saffron water, lemon juice, minced garlic, ground cumin, ground coriander, salt, and pepper until well combined.
3. **Marinate the Chicken:** Add the chicken thighs to the marinade, ensuring they are fully coated. Cover the bowl with plastic wrap or transfer to an airtight container. Marinate in the refrigerator for at least 2 hours, preferably overnight for deeper flavor.
4. **Preheat the Air Fryer:** Preheat your air fryer to 375°F (190°C).
5. **Cook the Chicken:** Remove the chicken thighs from the marinade, allowing any excess to drip off. Place them in the air fryer basket in a single layer. Cook at 375°F for 15-18 minutes, flipping halfway through, until the chicken is cooked through and the internal temperature reaches 165°F (74°C).
6. **Serve:** Remove the chicken from the air fryer and let it rest for a few minutes before serving. Garnish with fresh cilantro if desired.
7. **Serve warm:** Serve with rice, naan, or a fresh salad.

Servings: 4
Prep time: 10 minutes (plus marinating time)
Cooking time: 18 minutes

Nutritional info:
Calories: 250
Protein: 25g
Carbs: 5g
Fat: 14g

Quick tips:

- **Maximize Flavor:** For the best flavor, marinate the chicken overnight.
- **Make It Ahead:** You can prepare the marinade in advance and store it in the refrigerator for up to 2 days before using it.
- **Cooking Variation:** This marinade works well with chicken breasts or drumsticks too; just adjust the cooking time accordingly.

Lemongrass and Ginger Chicken Skewers

Lemongrass and Ginger Chicken Skewers are a light, flavorful dish perfect for grilling or air frying. The combination of fresh lemongrass, ginger, and garlic gives the chicken a bright and zesty taste, making these skewers ideal for a summer meal or appetizer.

Tools needed:

Air fryer
Skewers (metal or soaked wooden skewers)
Mixing bowl
Knife and cutting board
Grater or microplane for ginger

Ingredients:

- 2 boneless, skinless chicken breasts, cut into bite-sized pieces
- 2 stalks lemongrass, finely chopped
- 1 tbsp fresh ginger, grated
- 2 cloves garlic, minced
- 2 tbsp soy sauce
- 1 tbsp fish sauce
- 1 tbsp lime juice
- 1 tbsp honey
- 1 tbsp vegetable oil
- Fresh cilantro and lime wedges for garnish

Directions:

1. **Prepare the Marinade:** In a mixing bowl, combine the chopped lemongrass, grated ginger, minced garlic, soy sauce, fish sauce, lime juice, honey, and vegetable oil. Mix well to combine.
2. **Marinate the Chicken:** Add the chicken pieces to the marinade, tossing to coat evenly. Cover the bowl with plastic wrap and marinate in the refrigerator for at least 1 hour, or up to 4 hours for more intense flavor.
3. **Preheat the Air Fryer:** Preheat your air fryer to 375°F (190°C).
4. **Assemble the Skewers:** Thread the marinated chicken pieces onto the skewers, leaving a little space between each piece for even cooking.
5. **Cook the Skewers:** Place the skewers in the air fryer basket in a single layer. Cook at 375°F for 12-15 minutes, turning halfway through, until the chicken is cooked through and slightly charred on the edges.
6. **Serve:** Remove the skewers from the air fryer and let them rest for a few minutes. Garnish with fresh cilantro and serve with lime wedges on the side.
7. **Serve warm:** Enjoy as an appetizer or serve with rice or a salad for a complete meal.

Servings: 4 skewers
Prep time: 15 minutes (plus marinating time)
Cooking time: 15 minutes

Nutritional info: Calories: 200, Protein: 22g, Carbs: 8g, Fat: 10g

Quick tips:

- **Soak Wooden Skewers:** If using wooden skewers, soak them in water for at least 30 minutes before assembling to prevent them from burning.
- **Vegetable Additions:** Add pieces of bell pepper, onion, or pineapple to the skewers for extra flavor and texture.
- **Leftover Marinade:** Brush any leftover marinade onto the chicken during cooking for an extra burst of flavor.

Air Fryer Tandoori Cornish Hen

This Air Fryer Tandoori Cornish Hen is a flavorful and aromatic dish, marinated in a blend of yogurt and traditional Indian spices. The air fryer gives the hen a perfectly crispy exterior while keeping the meat juicy and tender. It's an impressive dish that's easy to prepare, ideal for a special dinner.

Tools needed:

Air fryer
Mixing bowl
Whisk or fork
Knife and cutting board
Basting brush
Meat thermometer

Ingredients:

- 1 Cornish hen, about 1-1.5 lbs
- 1/2 cup plain Greek yogurt
- 1 tbsp lemon juice
- 1 tbsp olive oil
- 2 cloves garlic, minced
- 1-inch piece of ginger, grated
- 1 tbsp tandoori masala or garam masala
- 1 tsp ground cumin
- 1 tsp ground coriander
- 1/2 tsp turmeric powder
- 1/2 tsp smoked paprika
- 1/4 tsp cayenne pepper (optional, for heat)
- Salt and pepper to taste
- Fresh cilantro and lemon wedges for garnish

Directions:

1. **Prepare the Marinade:** In a mixing bowl, whisk together the yogurt, lemon juice, olive oil, minced garlic, grated ginger, tandoori masala, cumin, coriander, turmeric, smoked paprika, cayenne pepper, salt, and pepper until well combined.
2. **Marinate the Cornish Hen:** Pat the Cornish hen dry with paper towels. Using a sharp knife, make a few slits on the skin to allow the marinade to penetrate. Rub the marinade all over the hen, making sure to coat it thoroughly, including the cavity. Cover the bowl with plastic wrap and marinate in the refrigerator for at least 4 hours, preferably overnight for deeper flavor.
3. **Preheat the Air Fryer:** Preheat your air fryer to 375°F (190°C).
4. **Cook the Cornish Hen:** Place the marinated Cornish hen in the air fryer basket, breast side down. Cook at 375°F for 25-30 minutes, flipping halfway through, until the skin is crispy and the internal temperature reaches 165°F (74°C).
5. **Rest and Serve:** Remove the Cornish hen from the air fryer and let it rest for 5 minutes before slicing. Garnish with fresh cilantro and serve with lemon wedges.
6. **Serve warm:** Pair with basmati rice or naan for a complete meal.

Servings: 2
Prep time: 15 minutes (plus marinating time)
Cooking time: 30 minutes

Nutritional info: Calories: 400, Protein: 35g, Carbs: 8g, Fat: 25g

Quick tips:

- **Enhanced Marination:** For a more intense flavor, marinate the Cornish hen overnight.
- **Even Cooking:** Ensure the Cornish hen is evenly coated with marinade to prevent any dry spots.
- **Cooking Variations:** This marinade also works well with chicken legs or thighs.

Persian-Spiced Chicken Wings with Pomegranate Molasses

These Persian-Spiced Chicken Wings are a deliciously exotic twist on a classic favorite. Marinated in a blend of Persian spices and glazed with sweet and tangy pomegranate molasses, these wings are bursting with flavor. Perfect for appetizers or a main dish.

Tools needed:

Air fryer
Mixing bowl
Whisk or fork
Basting brush
Knife and cutting board

Ingredients:

- 2 lbs chicken wings, separated into drumettes and flats
- 1 tbsp olive oil
- 1 tsp ground turmeric
- 1 tsp ground cumin
- 1 tsp ground coriander
- 1/2 tsp ground cinnamon
- 1/2 tsp ground cardamom
- 1/2 tsp ground allspice
- Salt and pepper to taste
- 1/4 cup pomegranate molasses
- 1 tbsp honey
- Fresh pomegranate seeds and chopped parsley for garnish

Directions:

1. **Prepare the Marinade:** In a mixing bowl, combine olive oil, turmeric, cumin, coriander, cinnamon, cardamom, allspice, salt, and pepper. Mix well to form a marinade.
2. **Marinate the Wings:** Add the chicken wings to the marinade, tossing to coat them evenly. Cover the bowl with plastic wrap and marinate in the refrigerator for at least 1 hour, or up to 4 hours for best results.
3. **Preheat the Air Fryer:** Preheat your air fryer to 375°F (190°C).
4. **Cook the Wings:** Arrange the marinated wings in a single layer in the air fryer basket. Cook at 375°F for 20-25 minutes, turning halfway through, until the wings are golden brown and crispy.
5. **Glaze the Wings:** While the wings are cooking, combine pomegranate molasses and honey in a small bowl. Once the wings are cooked, brush them with the pomegranate glaze and return them to the air fryer for an additional 3-5 minutes.
6. **Serve:** Remove the wings from the air fryer and transfer to a serving plate. Garnish with fresh pomegranate seeds and chopped parsley.
7. **Serve warm:** Enjoy these wings as an appetizer or serve with a side of rice or salad.

Servings: 4
Prep time: 15 minutes (plus marinating time)
Cooking time: 25 minutes

Nutritional info:
Calories: 280
Protein: 20g
Carbs: 10g
Fat: 18g

Quick tips:

- **Sticky Glaze:** For a thicker glaze, simmer the pomegranate molasses and honey mixture in a saucepan over low heat until it reduces slightly.
- **Make Ahead:** Marinate the wings the night before to save time and enhance the flavors.
- **Serving Suggestion:** Serve with a yogurt dipping sauce to balance the sweet and tangy flavors.

Air Fryer Chicken Livers with Herb Aioli

Air Fryer Chicken Livers are a quick, nutrient-dense dish that becomes a gourmet treat when paired with a creamy herb aioli. This recipe offers a perfect balance of crispiness and richness, ideal for appetizers or a light meal.

Tools needed:

Air fryer
Mixing bowl
Whisk or fork
Parchment paper or cooking spray
Knife and cutting board
Small bowl for aioli

Ingredients:

- 1 lb chicken livers, trimmed and cleaned
- 1/2 cup flour (optional, for a light coating)
- 1 tsp smoked paprika
- 1 tsp garlic powder
- 1/2 tsp ground black pepper
- Salt to taste
- Olive oil spray or 1 tbsp olive oil
- 1/2 cup mayonnaise
- 1 clove garlic, minced
- 1 tbsp fresh parsley, finely chopped
- 1 tbsp fresh chives, finely chopped
- 1 tsp lemon juice

Directions:

1. **Prepare the Chicken Livers:** Rinse the chicken livers under cold water and pat them dry with paper towels. Trim any excess fat or connective tissue.
2. **Season the Livers:** In a mixing bowl, combine the flour (if using), smoked paprika, garlic powder, black pepper, and salt. Toss the chicken livers in the mixture until evenly coated.
3. **Preheat the Air Fryer:** Preheat your air fryer to 375°F (190°C).
4. **Cook the Livers:** Lightly spray the air fryer basket with olive oil or line with parchment paper. Place the chicken livers in the basket in a single layer, making sure not to overcrowd them. Cook at 375°F for 10-12 minutes, shaking the basket halfway through, until the livers are golden brown and cooked through.
5. **Make the Herb Aioli:** While the livers are cooking, prepare the herb aioli by mixing the mayonnaise, minced garlic, parsley, chives, and lemon juice in a small bowl. Stir until well combined and smooth.
6. **Serve:** Remove the chicken livers from the air fryer and let them cool slightly. Serve with the herb aioli on the side for dipping.
7. **Serve warm:** Enjoy as an appetizer or with a side salad for a light meal.

Servings: 4
Prep time: 10 minutes
Cooking time: 12 minutes

Nutritional info:
Calories: 220
Protein: 18g
Carbs: 4g
Fat: 14g

Quick tips:

- **Lighter Option:** Skip the flour coating for a gluten-free and lighter version of the recipe.
- **Doneness Check:** Chicken livers should be slightly pink inside but not raw; overcooking can make them tough.
- **Herb Aioli:** The aioli can be made ahead and stored in the refrigerator for up to 3 days.

Crispy Chicken Skin Cracklings with Truffle Salt

Crispy Chicken Skin Cracklings are a savory and indulgent snack that's perfect for adding a gourmet touch to your appetizers or salads. The addition of truffle salt elevates the flavors, making these cracklings an irresistible treat.

Tools needed:

Air fryer
Knife and cutting board
Baking sheet
Parchment paper or aluminum foil
Small bowl

Ingredients:

- Chicken skin from 2-3 chicken breasts or thighs
- 1 tbsp olive oil
- 1/2 tsp truffle salt (or to taste)
- Freshly ground black pepper to taste
- Fresh herbs for garnish (optional)

Directions:

1. **Prepare the Chicken Skin:** Preheat your air fryer to 400°F (200°C). Lay the chicken skin flat on a cutting board and trim any excess fat. Pat the skin dry with paper towels to ensure it crisps up nicely.
2. **Season the Skin:** In a small bowl, toss the chicken skin with olive oil, truffle salt, and freshly ground black pepper. Make sure the skin is evenly coated.
3. **Cook the Chicken Skin:** Place the chicken skin in a single layer on a parchment-lined baking sheet or directly in the air fryer basket. Cook at 400°F for 8-10 minutes, or until the skin is golden brown and crispy. You may need to check halfway through and drain any excess fat.
4. **Cool and Serve:** Remove the cracklings from the air fryer and transfer them to a plate lined with paper towels to drain any remaining fat. Let them cool slightly to crisp up further.
5. **Serve:** Serve the cracklings as a snack, appetizer, or as a crispy topping for salads or soups. Garnish with fresh herbs if desired.
6. **Serve immediately:** Enjoy while warm for the best texture and flavor.

Servings: 2
Prep time: 5 minutes
Cooking time: 10 minutes

Nutritional info:
Calories: 150
Protein: 8g
Carbs: 0g
Fat: 14g

Quick tips:

- **Render Fat:** If the chicken skin releases too much fat during cooking, carefully drain it halfway through to keep the skin crispy.
- **Storage:** These cracklings are best enjoyed fresh, but they can be stored in an airtight container for up to 2 days.
- **Truffle Salt Substitute:** If you don't have truffle salt, you can use regular sea salt and add a drizzle of truffle oil after cooking.

Air Fryer Spatchcock Quail with Honey and Thyme

This Air Fryer Spatchcock Quail with Honey and Thyme is a delightful dish that combines the delicate flavor of quail with a sweet and herbaceous glaze. Spatchcocking the quail ensures even cooking, and the air fryer gives it a beautifully crispy skin.

Tools needed:

Air fryer
Sharp knife or kitchen shears
Basting brush
Small bowl
Meat thermometer

Ingredients:

- 2 whole quails, spatchcocked
- 2 tbsp olive oil
- 2 tbsp honey
- 1 tbsp fresh thyme leaves
- 1 tbsp lemon juice
- Salt and pepper to taste
- Lemon wedges for serving (optional)

Directions:

1. **Spatchcock the Quail:** To spatchcock the quail, place the bird breast side down on a cutting board. Using a sharp knife or kitchen shears, cut along both sides of the backbone and remove it. Flip the quail over and press down on the breastbone to flatten it. Repeat with the second quail.
2. **Preheat the Air Fryer:** Preheat your air fryer to 375°F (190°C).
3. **Season the Quail:** In a small bowl, mix the olive oil, honey, fresh thyme, lemon juice, salt, and pepper. Brush this mixture all over the quails, ensuring they are evenly coated.
4. **Cook the Quail:** Place the quails skin side up in the air fryer basket. Cook at 375°F for 12-15 minutes, until the skin is crispy and the internal temperature reaches 165°F (74°C). Baste the quails with the remaining honey and thyme mixture halfway through cooking for extra flavor.
5. **Rest and Serve:** Remove the quails from the air fryer and let them rest for a few minutes. Serve with lemon wedges on the side for a bright, fresh contrast.
6. **Serve warm:** Enjoy as a main dish with your favorite sides, such as roasted vegetables or a light salad.

Servings: 2
Prep time: 10 minutes
Cooking time: 15 minutes

Nutritional info:
Calories: 350
Protein: 20g
Carbs: 12g
Fat: 25g

Quick tips:

- **Even Cooking:** Spatchcocking the quail ensures even cooking and crispier skin. It also allows the quail to cook faster.
- **Honey Glaze:** For a deeper flavor, consider using a darker honey or adding a pinch of smoked paprika to the glaze.
- **Serving Suggestion:** Pair with a light grain like couscous or a refreshing cucumber salad to balance the richness of the quail.

AIRFRYER PORK RECIPES

Air Fryer Char Siu Pork Belly

Char Siu Pork Belly is a popular Chinese dish known for its sweet, savory, and sticky glaze. This air fryer version of the classic dish ensures that the pork belly is tender with a beautifully caramelized exterior. It's perfect for a flavorful and indulgent meal.

Tools needed:

Air fryer
Mixing bowl
Basting brush
Knife and cutting board
Aluminum foil

Ingredients:

- 1 lb pork belly, skin removed and cut into 1-inch thick strips
- 3 tbsp hoisin sauce
- 2 tbsp honey
- 2 tbsp soy sauce
- 1 tbsp oyster sauce
- 1 tbsp Shaoxing wine (or dry sherry)
- 1 tbsp dark soy sauce
- 1 tsp five-spice powder
- 2 cloves garlic, minced
- 1 tsp grated ginger
- 1/2 tsp red food coloring (optional, for traditional appearance)

Directions:

1. **Prepare the Marinade:** In a mixing bowl, combine hoisin sauce, honey, soy sauce, oyster sauce, Shaoxing wine, dark soy sauce, five-spice powder, minced garlic, grated ginger, and red food coloring (if using). Mix well to create the marinade.
2. **Marinate the Pork Belly:** Add the pork belly strips to the marinade, ensuring they are thoroughly coated. Cover and refrigerate for at least 4 hours, preferably overnight for the best flavor.
3. **Preheat the Air Fryer:** Preheat your air fryer to 375°F (190°C).
4. **Cook the Pork Belly:** Line the air fryer basket with aluminum foil to catch any drippings. Arrange the pork belly strips in a single layer in the basket. Cook at 375°F for 20-25 minutes, turning and basting with leftover marinade halfway through, until the pork belly is cooked through and caramelized.
5. **Rest and Serve:** Remove the pork belly from the air fryer and let it rest for a few minutes before slicing. The pork should be tender with a sticky glaze.
6. **Serve warm:** Serve with steamed rice and stir-fried vegetables for a complete meal.

Servings: 4
Prep time: 15 minutes (plus marinating time)
Cooking time: 25 minutes

Nutritional info: Calories: 400, Protein: 18g, Carbs: 15g, Fat: 30g

Quick tips:

- **Marination:** For the most authentic flavor, marinate the pork belly overnight.
- **Resting:** Allowing the pork to rest after cooking helps retain its juices, making it more tender.
- **Serving Suggestion:** Drizzle any leftover marinade over the pork belly before serving for extra flavor.

Vietnamese Lemongrass Pork Skewers

Vietnamese Lemongrass Pork Skewers are a flavorful and aromatic dish, perfect for grilling or air frying. The pork is marinated in a fragrant blend of lemongrass, garlic, and fish sauce, resulting in tender, juicy skewers with a deliciously charred exterior.

Tools needed:

Air fryer
Skewers (metal or soaked wooden skewers)
Mixing bowl
Knife and cutting board
Grater or microplane for lemongrass and ginger

Ingredients:

- 1 lb pork shoulder or pork loin, thinly sliced
- 2 stalks lemongrass, finely chopped
- 2 cloves garlic, minced
- 1 tbsp fresh ginger, grated
- 2 tbsp fish sauce
- 1 tbsp soy sauce
- 1 tbsp sugar
- 1 tbsp vegetable oil
- 1 tbsp lime juice
- Fresh cilantro and lime wedges for garnish

Directions:

1. **Prepare the Marinade:** In a mixing bowl, combine the chopped lemongrass, minced garlic, grated ginger, fish sauce, soy sauce, sugar, vegetable oil, and lime juice. Mix well to create the marinade.
2. **Marinate the Pork:** Add the sliced pork to the marinade, tossing to coat evenly. Cover and refrigerate for at least 1 hour, or up to 4 hours for the best flavor.
3. **Preheat the Air Fryer:** Preheat your air fryer to 375°F (190°C).
4. **Assemble the Skewers:** Thread the marinated pork slices onto the skewers, leaving a little space between each piece for even cooking.
5. **Cook the Skewers:** Arrange the skewers in a single layer in the air fryer basket. Cook at 375°F for 12-15 minutes, turning halfway through, until the pork is cooked through and slightly charred on the edges.
6. **Serve:** Remove the skewers from the air fryer and let them rest for a few minutes. Garnish with fresh cilantro and serve with lime wedges.
7. **Serve warm:** Enjoy as an appetizer or pair with rice noodles and fresh vegetables for a complete meal.

Servings: 4 skewers
Prep time: 15 minutes (plus marinating time)
Cooking time: 15 minutes

Nutritional info:
Calories: 250
Protein: 22g
Carbs: 7g
Fat: 14g

Quick tips:

- **Soak Wooden Skewers:** If using wooden skewers, soak them in water for at least 30 minutes before assembling to prevent burning.
- **Lemongrass Preparation:** Make sure to use only the tender inner parts of the lemongrass stalks for the marinade.
- **Serving Suggestion:** Serve with a side of pickled vegetables and rice for an authentic Vietnamese experience.

Air Fryer Porchetta with Fennel and Garlic

Porchetta is a traditional Italian dish made from a pork roast that's been seasoned with herbs and spices, then slow-roasted until tender. This air fryer version delivers all the rich flavors of porchetta in less time, with a crispy, crackling skin and succulent, juicy meat.

Tools needed:

Air fryer
Knife and cutting board
Butcher's twine
Basting brush
Meat thermometer

Ingredients:

- 2 lb pork belly, skin on
- 2 tbsp olive oil
- 4 cloves garlic, minced
- 1 tbsp fennel seeds, toasted and crushed
- 1 tbsp fresh rosemary, finely chopped
- 1 tbsp fresh thyme leaves
- 1 tsp ground black pepper
- 1 tsp red pepper flakes (optional, for heat)
- Zest of 1 lemon
- 1 tbsp kosher salt

Directions:

1. **Prepare the Pork Belly:** Lay the pork belly skin side down on a cutting board. Score the meat with a sharp knife, making shallow cuts in a crisscross pattern. This will help the seasoning penetrate deeper.
2. **Make the Herb Mixture:** In a small bowl, mix together the minced garlic, fennel seeds, rosemary, thyme, black pepper, red pepper flakes (if using), lemon zest, and kosher salt. Rub this mixture all over the scored side of the pork belly.
3. **Roll and Tie the Pork:** Roll the pork belly tightly, with the skin on the outside, and secure it with butcher's twine at 1-inch intervals to maintain its shape.
4. **Preheat the Air Fryer:** Preheat your air fryer to 375°F (190°C).
5. **Cook the Porchetta:** Brush the skin of the pork belly with olive oil and place the rolled pork belly in the air fryer basket, seam side down. Cook at 375°F for 30-35 minutes, then increase the temperature to 400°F (200°C) and cook for an additional 10-15 minutes to crisp up the skin. The internal temperature should reach 145°F (63°C).
6. **Rest and Serve:** Remove the porchetta from the air fryer and let it rest for 10 minutes before slicing. This allows the juices to redistribute, making the meat more tender.
7. **Serve:** Slice the porchetta into rounds and serve with roasted vegetables or a fresh salad.

Servings: 4 | **Prep time:** 20 minutes | **Cooking time:** 45-50 minutes

Nutritional info: Calories: 500, Protein: 25g, Carbs: 1g, Fat: 45g
Quick tips:

- **Crispier Skin:** To ensure extra crispy skin, pat the pork belly dry with paper towels before seasoning and let it air-dry in the refrigerator uncovered for a few hours or overnight.
- **Leftovers:** Leftover porchetta makes for delicious sandwiches or can be added to pasta dishes.
- **Cooking Variation:** If the pork belly is thick, you may need to cook it slightly longer.

Coffee-Crusted Pork Tenderloin

This Coffee-Crusted Pork Tenderloin is a bold and flavorful dish that combines the rich, earthy notes of coffee with the tender juiciness of pork. The coffee crust creates a beautifully seared exterior while locking in the moisture of the meat, making it an ideal choice for a special dinner.

Tools needed:

Air fryer
Mixing bowl
Basting brush
Meat thermometer
Knife and cutting board

Ingredients:

- 1 lb pork tenderloin
- 2 tbsp ground coffee (medium to coarse grind)
- 1 tbsp brown sugar
- 1 tsp smoked paprika
- 1/2 tsp ground cumin
- 1/2 tsp ground coriander
- 1/2 tsp garlic powder
- 1/2 tsp salt
- 1/4 tsp ground black pepper
- 1 tbsp olive oil

Directions:

1. **Prepare the Coffee Rub:** In a mixing bowl, combine ground coffee, brown sugar, smoked paprika, ground cumin, ground coriander, garlic powder, salt, and black pepper. Mix well.
2. **Season the Pork Tenderloin:** Pat the pork tenderloin dry with paper towels. Rub the olive oil all over the tenderloin, then coat it generously with the coffee rub, pressing the spices into the meat to ensure an even coating.
3. **Preheat the Air Fryer:** Preheat your air fryer to 375°F (190°C).
4. **Cook the Pork Tenderloin:** Place the seasoned pork tenderloin in the air fryer basket. Cook at 375°F for 20-25 minutes, turning halfway through, until the internal temperature reaches 145°F (63°C) for medium-rare or 160°F (71°C) for medium.
5. **Rest and Serve:** Remove the pork tenderloin from the air fryer and let it rest for 5-10 minutes before slicing. This helps the juices redistribute throughout the meat, making it more tender.
6. **Serve:** Slice the pork tenderloin into medallions and serve with roasted vegetables or a fresh salad.

Servings: 4
Prep time: 10 minutes
Cooking time: 25 minutes

Nutritional info:
Calories: 240
Protein: 28g
Carbs: 4g
Fat: 12g

Quick tips:

- **Even Coating:** Ensure the coffee rub is evenly distributed on the pork for a consistent crust.
- **Resting:** Allow the pork to rest after cooking to enhance tenderness and flavor.
- **Serving Suggestion:** Pair with a red wine reduction sauce for an extra layer of flavor.

Air Fryer Pork Satay with Peanut Sauce

Pork Satay is a popular Southeast Asian dish featuring marinated and skewered pork, grilled to perfection and served with a rich, creamy peanut sauce.

Tools needed:

Air fryer
Skewers (metal or soaked wooden skewers)
Mixing bowl
Knife and cutting board
Small saucepan for peanut sauce

Ingredients:

- 1 lb pork shoulder or pork loin, thinly sliced
- 2 tbsp soy sauce
- 1 tbsp fish sauce
- 1 tbsp brown sugar
- 1 tbsp vegetable oil
- 1 clove garlic, minced
- 1 tsp ground coriander
- 1 tsp ground turmeric
- 1/2 tsp ground cumin
- 1/2 tsp ground ginger

For the Peanut Sauce:

- 1/4 cup creamy peanut butter
- 1 tbsp soy sauce
- 1 tbsp lime juice
- 1 tbsp honey
- 1/2 cup coconut milk
- 1/2 tsp red pepper flakes (optional, for heat)

Directions:

Prepare the Marinade: In a mixing bowl, combine soy sauce, fish sauce, brown sugar, vegetable oil, minced garlic, ground coriander, turmeric, cumin, and ginger. Mix well.

Marinate the Pork: Add the sliced pork to the marinade, tossing to coat evenly. Cover and refrigerate for at least 1 hour, or up to 4 hours for best results.

Preheat the Air Fryer: Preheat your air fryer to 375°F (190°C).

Assemble the Skewers: Thread the marinated pork slices onto the skewers, leaving a little space between each piece for even cooking.

Cook the Skewers: Arrange the skewers in a single layer in the air fryer basket. Cook at 375°F for 10-12 minutes, turning halfway through, until the pork is cooked through and slightly charred on the edges.

Make the Peanut Sauce: While the pork is cooking, prepare the peanut sauce. In a small saucepan, combine peanut butter, soy sauce, lime juice, honey, coconut milk, and red pepper flakes (if using). Heat over low heat, stirring until the sauce is smooth and well combined. Adjust seasoning to taste.

Serve: Remove the pork satay from the air fryer and serve with the warm peanut sauce on the side.

Serve warm: Enjoy as an appetizer or pair with jasmine rice and fresh cucumber slices for a complete meal.

Servings: 4 skewers | **Prep time:** 15 minutes (plus marinating time) | **Cooking time:** 12 minutes

Nutritional info: Calories: 320, Protein: 25g, Carbs: 10g, Fat: 20g

Quick tips:

- **Skewer Tips:** If using wooden skewers, soak them in water for at least 30 minutes before threading the pork to prevent burning.
- **Peanut Sauce Consistency:** Adjust the thickness of the peanut sauce by adding more coconut milk if needed.
- **Serving Suggestion:** Serve with a fresh herb garnish, such as cilantro or Thai basil, to enhance the flavors.

Sichuan Peppercorn and Honey-Glazed Pork Ribs

These Sichuan Peppercorn and Honey-Glazed Pork Ribs are a mouthwatering combination of sweet, spicy, and numbing flavors. The Sichuan peppercorns add a unique tingly sensation, while the honey glaze provides a perfect balance of sweetness, making these ribs a showstopper at any meal.

Tools needed:

Air fryer
Mixing bowl
Basting brush
Meat thermometer
Knife and cutting board

Ingredients:

- 1.5 lbs pork ribs, cut into individual ribs
- 1 tbsp Sichuan peppercorns, toasted and crushed
- 2 tbsp soy sauce
- 2 tbsp rice vinegar
- 2 tbsp honey
- 1 tbsp hoisin sauce
- 2 cloves garlic, minced
- 1-inch piece of ginger, grated
- 1 tsp five-spice powder
- 1 tsp chili flakes (optional, for heat)
- 1 tbsp sesame oil
- Fresh cilantro and sesame seeds for garnish

Directions:

1. **Prepare the Marinade:** In a mixing bowl, combine crushed Sichuan peppercorns, soy sauce, rice vinegar, honey, hoisin sauce, minced garlic, grated ginger, five-spice powder, chili flakes (if using), and sesame oil. Mix well.
2. **Marinate the Ribs:** Add the pork ribs to the marinade, ensuring they are well coated. Cover and refrigerate for at least 2 hours, or overnight for maximum flavor.
3. **Preheat the Air Fryer:** Preheat your air fryer to 375°F (190°C).
4. **Cook the Ribs:** Place the marinated ribs in the air fryer basket in a single layer. Cook at 375°F for 25-30 minutes, turning and basting with any remaining marinade halfway through, until the ribs are tender and caramelized. The internal temperature should reach at least 145°F (63°C).
5. **Glaze the Ribs:** In the last 5 minutes of cooking, brush the ribs with additional honey for a sticky glaze.
6. **Serve:** Remove the ribs from the air fryer and let them rest for a few minutes. Garnish with fresh cilantro and sesame seeds.
7. **Serve warm:** Enjoy as a main dish with steamed rice or a fresh salad.

Servings: 4
Prep time: 15 minutes (plus marinating time)
Cooking time: 30 minutes

Nutritional info: Calories: 400, Protein: 25g, Carbs: 20g, Fat: 25g

Quick tips:

- **Toasting Peppercorns:** Toast the Sichuan peppercorns in a dry skillet over medium heat until fragrant before crushing them. This enhances their flavor.
- **Sticky Glaze:** For an extra-sticky finish, increase the honey in the glaze during the final basting.
- **Serving Suggestion:** Pair with a simple cucumber salad or pickled vegetables to balance the richness of the ribs.

Air Fryer Pancetta-Wrapped Scallops

Air Fryer Pancetta-Wrapped Scallops are a luxurious appetizer that combines the delicate sweetness of scallops with the salty, savory flavor of pancetta. The air fryer ensures the pancetta becomes crispy while the scallops remain tender and juicy, making this dish perfect for entertaining.

Tools needed:

Air fryer
Toothpicks
Basting brush
Knife and cutting board
Small bowl

Ingredients:

- 12 large sea scallops, cleaned and patted dry
- 6 slices pancetta, thinly sliced and cut in half
- 1 tbsp olive oil
- 1 tbsp lemon juice
- 1 clove garlic, minced
- Freshly ground black pepper to taste
- Fresh parsley for garnish (optional)
- Lemon wedges for serving (optional)

Directions:

1. **Prepare the Scallops:** Pat the scallops dry with paper towels to remove any excess moisture. Season them lightly with black pepper.
2. **Wrap the Scallops:** Wrap each scallop with a half slice of pancetta, securing it with a toothpick. Make sure the pancetta is tightly wrapped around the scallop to prevent it from unraveling during cooking.
3. **Prepare the Marinade:** In a small bowl, mix together olive oil, lemon juice, and minced garlic. Brush this mixture over the pancetta-wrapped scallops.
4. **Preheat the Air Fryer:** Preheat your air fryer to 400°F (200°C).
5. **Cook the Scallops:** Place the scallops in the air fryer basket in a single layer. Cook at 400°F for 8-10 minutes, turning halfway through, until the pancetta is crispy and the scallops are opaque and cooked through.
6. **Serve:** Remove the scallops from the air fryer and let them rest for a minute. Garnish with fresh parsley and serve with lemon wedges if desired.
7. **Serve immediately:** These scallops are best enjoyed hot and fresh.

Servings: 4
Prep time: 10 minutes
Cooking time: 10 minutes

Nutritional info:
Calories: 120
Protein: 10g
Carbs: 1g
Fat: 8g

Quick tips:

- **Avoid Overcooking:** Scallops cook quickly, so keep an eye on them to avoid overcooking, which can make them tough.
- **Even Wrapping:** Ensure the pancetta is evenly wrapped around each scallop for consistent cooking.
- **Serving Suggestion:** Pair with a light salad or serve as a starter for a special meal.

Bacon-Wrapped Dates Stuffed with Blue Cheese

Bacon-Wrapped Dates Stuffed with Blue Cheese are an irresistible combination of sweet, savory, and creamy flavors. The smoky bacon, sweet dates, and tangy blue cheese create a perfect balance, making these bites a crowd-pleasing appetizer that's both simple and elegant.

Tools needed:

Air fryer
Toothpicks
Knife and cutting board
Small spoon

Ingredients:

- 12 Medjool dates, pitted
- 12 small cubes of blue cheese (about 1/2 inch in size)
- 6 slices of bacon, cut in half
- Freshly ground black pepper to taste
- Fresh parsley for garnish (optional)

Directions:

1. **Prepare the Dates:** Slice each date lengthwise on one side and gently open it up to create a pocket. Insert a cube of blue cheese into each date, then press the date back together to enclose the cheese.
2. **Wrap the Dates:** Wrap each stuffed date with a half slice of bacon, securing it with a toothpick. Make sure the bacon is snugly wrapped around the date to hold everything in place.
3. **Preheat the Air Fryer:** Preheat your air fryer to 375°F (190°C).
4. **Cook the Dates:** Place the bacon-wrapped dates in the air fryer basket in a single layer. Cook at 375°F for 10-12 minutes, turning halfway through, until the bacon is crispy and the dates are heated through.
5. **Serve:** Remove the dates from the air fryer and let them cool slightly before serving. Garnish with freshly ground black pepper and parsley if desired.
6. **Serve immediately:** Enjoy these dates warm as a delightful appetizer.

Servings: 4
Prep time: 10 minutes
Cooking time: 12 minutes

Nutritional info:
Calories: 150
Protein: 4g
Carbs: 15g
Fat: 9g

Quick tips:

- **Secure Wrapping:** Use toothpicks to secure the bacon around the dates to prevent them from unraveling during cooking.
- **Cheese Substitution:** If you're not a fan of blue cheese, try stuffing the dates with goat cheese or cream cheese for a milder flavor.
- **Serving Suggestion:** These dates pair well with sparkling wine or a crisp white wine, making them perfect for holiday parties or special occasions.

Air Fryer Crispy Fish Skin Chips with Lime Salt

Crispy Fish Skin Chips are a delightful, crunchy snack that's packed with flavor and nutrition. The fish skin is air-fried to a perfect crispness, then dusted with a zesty lime salt, making these chips a unique and addictive treat.

Tools needed:

Air fryer
Knife and cutting board
Baking sheet
Parchment paper
Zester or microplane
Small bowl

Ingredients:

- Fish skin from 2-3 fillets (such as salmon, trout, or snapper), cleaned and patted dry
- 1 tbsp olive oil
- Zest of 1 lime
- 1 tsp sea salt
- 1/2 tsp smoked paprika (optional)
- Fresh lime wedges for serving (optional)

Directions:

1. **Prepare the Fish Skin:** Preheat your air fryer to 400°F (200°C). Lay the fish skin flat on a cutting board and scrape off any remaining flesh or fat with a knife. Pat the skin dry with paper towels to ensure it crisps up nicely.
2. **Season the Skin:** Rub the fish skin with olive oil, ensuring it's evenly coated. Place the skins on a parchment-lined baking sheet, skin side up.
3. **Cook the Fish Skin:** Place the fish skins in the air fryer basket in a single layer. Cook at 400°F for 6-8 minutes, or until the skins are golden brown and crispy. Check halfway through and adjust the time as needed to prevent burning.
4. **Make the Lime Salt:** While the skins are cooking, combine the lime zest, sea salt, and smoked paprika (if using) in a small bowl.
5. **Season the Chips:** Once the fish skins are done, transfer them to a plate and sprinkle immediately with the lime salt mixture.
6. **Serve:** Serve the crispy fish skin chips with fresh lime wedges on the side for an extra burst of citrus.
7. **Serve immediately:** Enjoy as a snack or as a crunchy topping for salads and soups.

Servings: 2
Prep time: 10 minutes
Cooking time: 8 minutes

Nutritional info:
Calories: 100
Protein: 8g
Carbs: 0g
Fat: 8g

Quick tips:

- **Crispy Texture:** Ensure the fish skin is completely dry before cooking for the crispiest results.
- **Lime Salt:** Make extra lime salt and store it in an airtight container for future use on popcorn, fries, or grilled vegetables.
- **Serving Suggestion:** Pair these chips with a cold beer or a light white wine for a refreshing snack.

Wasabi-Crusted Salmon with Pickled Ginger

Wasabi-Crusted Salmon is a bold, flavorful dish that combines the heat of wasabi with the richness of salmon. Topped with pickled ginger, this dish offers a perfect balance of flavors and textures, making it an impressive and satisfying main course.

Tools needed:

Air fryer
Small mixing bowl
Basting brush
Knife and cutting board
Small bowl

Ingredients:

- 2 salmon fillets, skin on
- 2 tbsp wasabi paste
- 1/4 cup panko breadcrumbs
- 1 tbsp sesame seeds
- 1 tbsp soy sauce
- 1 tbsp honey
- 1 tbsp olive oil
- Pickled ginger, for serving
- Fresh cilantro or scallions for garnish (optional)

Directions:

1. **Prepare the Salmon:** Pat the salmon fillets dry with paper towels. In a small bowl, mix together the wasabi paste, soy sauce, and honey. Brush this mixture evenly over the tops of the salmon fillets.
2. **Make the Crust:** In another small bowl, combine the panko breadcrumbs and sesame seeds. Press this mixture onto the wasabi-coated side of the salmon fillets to create a crust.
3. **Preheat the Air Fryer:** Preheat your air fryer to 375°F (190°C).
4. **Cook the Salmon:** Place the salmon fillets, skin side down, in the air fryer basket. Cook at 375°F for 10-12 minutes, or until the salmon is cooked through and the crust is golden brown.
5. **Serve:** Remove the salmon from the air fryer and let it rest for a minute. Top with pickled ginger and garnish with fresh cilantro or scallions if desired.
6. **Serve immediately:** Pair with steamed rice or a fresh salad for a complete meal.

Servings: 2
Prep time: 10 minutes
Cooking time: 12 minutes

Nutritional info:
Calories: 350
Protein: 30g
Carbs: 10g
Fat: 20g

Quick tips:

- **Adjust Heat:** If you prefer a milder flavor, reduce the amount of wasabi or mix it with more honey.
- **Crispier Crust:** For an extra-crispy crust, spray the top of the salmon with a light mist of oil before cooking.
- **Serving Suggestion:** Serve with a side of sautéed greens or a cucumber salad to complement the flavors.

Air Fryer Stuffed Squid with Chorizo and Rice

Air Fryer Stuffed Squid with Chorizo and Rice is a flavorful and unique dish that brings together the tender, mild taste of squid with a rich and spicy chorizo and rice stuffing. This dish is perfect for impressing guests with its gourmet appeal and bold flavors.

Tools needed:

Air fryer
Mixing bowl
Skillet
Toothpicks
Knife and cutting board

Ingredients:

- 4 medium squid tubes, cleaned
- 1/2 cup cooked rice
- 1/4 cup diced chorizo sausage
- 1/4 cup finely chopped onion
- 2 cloves garlic, minced
- 1/4 cup diced tomatoes
- 1 tbsp olive oil
- 1 tbsp fresh parsley, chopped
- 1/2 tsp smoked paprika
- Salt and pepper to taste
- Lemon wedges for serving

Directions:

1. **Prepare the Stuffing:** Heat the olive oil in a skillet over medium heat. Add the diced chorizo, onion, and garlic, and sauté until the onion is soft and the chorizo is browned, about 5 minutes. Stir in the diced tomatoes, cooked rice, smoked paprika, salt, and pepper. Cook for another 2 minutes, then remove from heat and stir in the chopped parsley.
2. **Stuff the Squid:** Carefully stuff each squid tube with the chorizo and rice mixture, leaving a little room at the top to close the opening. Secure the open end with toothpicks to prevent the filling from spilling out.
3. **Preheat the Air Fryer:** Preheat your air fryer to 375°F (190°C).
4. **Cook the Squid:** Lightly brush the stuffed squid with olive oil and place them in the air fryer basket. Cook at 375°F for 10-12 minutes, turning halfway through, until the squid is cooked through and slightly golden.
5. **Serve:** Remove the squid from the air fryer and let them rest for a minute. Remove the toothpicks before serving.
6. **Serve immediately:** Serve with lemon wedges on the side for a fresh citrus finish.

Servings: 4
Prep time: 15 minutes
Cooking time: 12 minutes

Nutritional info:
Calories: 220
Protein: 15g
Carbs: 10g
Fat: 12g

Quick tips:

- **Prevent Overstuffing:** Don't overfill the squid tubes, as the filling can expand during cooking and cause the squid to split.
- **Toothpicks:** Use wooden toothpicks for securing the squid, and be sure to remove them before serving.
- **Serving Suggestion:** Pair with a simple green salad or roasted vegetables for a complete meal.

Spiced Mackerel with Tamarind and Fennel

Spiced Mackerel with Tamarind and Fennel is a flavorful and aromatic dish that brings together the rich taste of mackerel with a tangy tamarind glaze and the subtle sweetness of fennel. This dish is perfect for those who enjoy bold, vibrant flavors in their seafood.

Tools needed:

Air fryer
Small mixing bowl
Basting brush
Knife and cutting board
Small saucepan

Ingredients:

- 2 whole mackerel, cleaned and gutted
- 2 tbsp tamarind paste
- 1 tbsp honey
- 1 tsp ground fennel seeds
- 1 tsp ground coriander
- 1/2 tsp ground cumin
- 1/2 tsp turmeric powder
- 1/4 tsp cayenne pepper (optional, for heat)
- 1 tbsp olive oil
- Salt and pepper to taste
- Fresh fennel fronds or cilantro for garnish
- Lemon wedges for serving

Directions:

1. **Prepare the Spice Mix:** In a small mixing bowl, combine the tamarind paste, honey, ground fennel seeds, coriander, cumin, turmeric, cayenne pepper (if using), and olive oil. Mix well to form a thick paste.
2. **Season the Mackerel:** Pat the mackerel dry with paper towels. Make a few diagonal slashes on each side of the fish to allow the marinade to penetrate. Rub the tamarind spice paste all over the mackerel, including inside the cavity. Let it marinate for at least 15 minutes.
3. **Preheat the Air Fryer:** Preheat your air fryer to 375°F (190°C).
4. **Cook the Mackerel:** Place the mackerel in the air fryer basket, making sure they are not overcrowded. Cook at 375°F for 10-12 minutes, turning halfway through, until the fish is cooked through and the skin is slightly charred and crispy.
5. **Serve:** Remove the mackerel from the air fryer and let them rest for a minute. Garnish with fresh fennel fronds or cilantro and serve with lemon wedges.
6. **Serve immediately:** Enjoy as a main dish with rice or a light salad.

Servings: 2
Prep time: 15 minutes
Cooking time: 12 minutes

Nutritional info:
Calories: 320
Protein: 25g
Carbs: 10g
Fat: 20g

Quick tips:

- **Avoid Overcrowding:** Cook the mackerel in batches if necessary to ensure even cooking.
- **Tamarind Paste:** Adjust the amount of tamarind paste based on your preference for tanginess.
- **Serving Suggestion:** Serve with a side of pickled vegetables or a cooling yogurt sauce to balance the spices.

Air Fryer Clam Cakes with Lemon Aioli

Air Fryer Clam Cakes are a delightful New England-inspired snack or appetizer, combining tender clams with a light and crispy batter.

Tools needed:

Air fryer
Mixing bowl
Whisk or fork
Spoon or small ice cream scoop
Knife and cutting board
Small bowl for aioli

Ingredients:

- 1 cup all-purpose flour
- 1 tsp baking powder
- 1/2 tsp Old Bay seasoning
- 1/4 tsp salt
- 1/4 cup milk
- 1 large egg
- 1/2 cup chopped clams (fresh or canned)
- 1 tbsp fresh parsley, chopped
- 1 tbsp melted butter
- Olive oil spray

For the Lemon Aioli:

- 1/4 cup mayonnaise
- 1 tbsp lemon juice
- 1 tsp lemon zest
- 1 clove garlic, minced
- Salt and pepper to taste

Directions:

1. **Prepare the Batter:** In a mixing bowl, whisk together the flour, baking powder, Old Bay seasoning, and salt. In another bowl, combine the milk, egg, and melted butter. Pour the wet ingredients into the dry ingredients and mix until just combined. Fold in the chopped clams and parsley.
2. **Preheat the Air Fryer:** Preheat your air fryer to 375°F (190°C).
3. **Form the Clam Cakes:** Using a spoon or small ice cream scoop, drop spoonfuls of the batter onto a parchment-lined air fryer basket. Lightly flatten each cake with the back of the spoon. Spray the tops with olive oil.
4. **Cook the Clam Cakes:** Cook the clam cakes at 375°F for 8-10 minutes, flipping halfway through, until golden brown and crispy.
5. **Make the Lemon Aioli:** While the clam cakes are cooking, prepare the lemon aioli by mixing mayonnaise, lemon juice, lemon zest, and minced garlic in a small bowl. Season with salt and pepper to taste.
6. **Serve:** Remove the clam cakes from the air fryer and let them cool slightly. Serve with lemon aioli on the side for dipping.
7. **Serve immediately:** Enjoy as a snack, appetizer, or alongside a fresh salad.

Servings: 4 | **Prep time:** 10 minutes | **Cooking time:** 10 minutes
Nutritional info: Calories: 250, Protein: 8g, Carbs: 20g, Fat: 15g

Quick tips:

- **Crispy Edges:** For extra crispy edges, spray the clam cakes with a little more olive oil before cooking.
- **Lemon Aioli:** Make the aioli ahead of time and store it in the refrigerator for up to 3 days.
- **Serving Suggestion:** Garnish with additional fresh parsley and serve with lemon wedges for an extra citrus kick.

Octopus and Potato Skewers with Smoked Paprika

Octopus and Potato Skewers with Smoked Paprika is a Spanish-inspired dish that combines tender octopus with creamy potatoes, all seasoned with smoky paprika. The air fryer ensures the skewers are perfectly cooked with a slightly crispy exterior, making this a delightful and unique appetizer or main course.

Tools needed:

Air fryer
Skewers (metal or soaked wooden skewers)
Large pot
Knife and cutting board
Mixing bowl

Ingredients:

- 1 lb cooked octopus, cut into bite-sized pieces
- 4 small potatoes, boiled and cut into chunks
- 1 tbsp olive oil
- 1 tsp smoked paprika
- 1 tsp garlic powder
- 1/2 tsp dried oregano
- Salt and pepper to taste
- Fresh parsley for garnish
- Lemon wedges for serving

Directions:

1. **Prepare the Ingredients:** Boil the potatoes until just tender, about 10 minutes. Drain and let them cool slightly. Cut the cooked octopus into bite-sized pieces.
2. **Season the Skewers:** In a mixing bowl, combine the octopus, boiled potatoes, olive oil, smoked paprika, garlic powder, oregano, salt, and pepper. Toss until everything is evenly coated.
3. **Assemble the Skewers:** Thread the seasoned octopus and potato chunks onto the skewers, alternating between the two.
4. **Preheat the Air Fryer:** Preheat your air fryer to 375°F (190°C).
5. **Cook the Skewers:** Place the skewers in the air fryer basket in a single layer. Cook at 375°F for 8-10 minutes, turning halfway through, until the potatoes are crispy and the octopus is slightly charred.
6. **Serve:** Remove the skewers from the air fryer and garnish with fresh parsley. Serve with lemon wedges on the side.
7. **Serve immediately:** Enjoy as an appetizer or pair with a light salad for a complete meal.

Servings: 4
Prep time: 15 minutes
Cooking time: 10 minutes

Nutritional info:
Calories: 200
Protein: 15g
Carbs: 18g
Fat: 8g

Quick tips:

- **Octopus Preparation:** Use pre-cooked octopus to save time, or cook the octopus beforehand by simmering in water for about 45 minutes until tender.
- **Crispy Potatoes:** Ensure the potatoes are fully cooked and slightly crispy before threading onto the skewers for the best texture.
- **Serving Suggestion:** Pair with a chilled white wine or a light, citrusy beer to complement the smoky flavors.

Air Fryer Turmeric-Crusted Cod

Air Fryer Turmeric-Crusted Cod is a vibrant and flavorful dish that features cod fillets coated in a fragrant turmeric and spice blend. The air fryer gives the fish a crispy exterior while keeping the inside tender and flaky, making it a healthy and delicious option for a quick meal.

Tools needed:

Air fryer
Mixing bowl
Basting brush
Knife and cutting board
Small bowl

Ingredients:

- 4 cod fillets, about 6 oz each
- 2 tbsp olive oil
- 1 tsp ground turmeric
- 1/2 tsp ground cumin
- 1/2 tsp ground coriander
- 1/4 tsp smoked paprika
- 1/4 tsp garlic powder
- Salt and pepper to taste
- Lemon wedges for serving
- Fresh cilantro for garnish (optional)

Directions:

1. **Prepare the Spice Rub:** In a small bowl, mix together the turmeric, cumin, coriander, smoked paprika, garlic powder, salt, and pepper.
2. **Season the Cod:** Pat the cod fillets dry with paper towels. Brush both sides of the fillets with olive oil, then rub the spice mixture evenly over each fillet.
3. **Preheat the Air Fryer:** Preheat your air fryer to 375°F (190°C).
4. **Cook the Cod:** Place the cod fillets in the air fryer basket in a single layer. Cook at 375°F for 8-10 minutes, or until the fish is golden brown and cooked through. The internal temperature should reach 145°F (63°C).
5. **Serve:** Remove the cod from the air fryer and let it rest for a minute. Garnish with fresh cilantro and serve with lemon wedges.
6. **Serve immediately:** Pair with steamed vegetables or a fresh salad for a complete meal.

Servings: 4
Prep time: 10 minutes
Cooking time: 10 minutes

Nutritional info:
Calories: 180
Protein: 24g
Carbs: 2g
Fat: 8g

Quick tips:

- **Even Coating:** Ensure the spice rub is evenly distributed on the fish for consistent flavor.
- **Serving Suggestion:** Serve with a side of basmati rice or quinoa to complement the flavors.
- **Turmeric Staining:** Be careful when handling turmeric as it can stain surfaces and clothing. Use gloves if needed.

Coconut-Lime Shrimp with Mango Salsa

Coconut-Lime Shrimp with Mango Salsa is a tropical-inspired dish that pairs crispy coconut-coated shrimp with a refreshing and sweet mango salsa. The combination of flavors and textures makes this dish perfect for a light and vibrant meal or appetizer.

Tools needed:

Air fryer
Mixing bowls
Basting brush
Knife and cutting board
Small whisk

Ingredients:

- 1 lb large shrimp, peeled and deveined
- 1/2 cup unsweetened shredded coconut
- 1/4 cup panko breadcrumbs
- 2 tbsp flour
- 2 large eggs, beaten
- 1 tbsp lime juice
- 1 tsp lime zest
- Salt and pepper to taste
- Olive oil spray

For the Mango Salsa:

- 1 ripe mango, diced
- 1/4 cup red bell pepper, diced
- 1/4 cup red onion, finely chopped
- 1 tbsp fresh cilantro, chopped
- 1 tbsp lime juice
- 1 tsp honey
- Salt and pepper to taste

Directions:

1. **Prepare the Shrimp Coating:** In a mixing bowl, combine the shredded coconut, panko breadcrumbs, lime zest, salt, and pepper. In a separate bowl, place the flour. In another bowl, beat the eggs with lime juice.
2. **Coat the Shrimp:** Dredge each shrimp in the flour, then dip it into the beaten eggs, and finally coat it with the coconut-panko mixture, pressing lightly to adhere.
3. **Preheat the Air Fryer:** Preheat your air fryer to 375°F (190°C).
4. **Cook the Shrimp:** Arrange the coated shrimp in the air fryer basket in a single layer. Lightly spray with olive oil. Cook at 375°F for 6-8 minutes, turning halfway through, until the shrimp are golden brown and crispy.
5. **Prepare the Mango Salsa:** While the shrimp are cooking, combine the diced mango, red bell pepper, red onion, cilantro, lime juice, honey, salt, and pepper in a mixing bowl. Stir gently to combine.
6. **Serve:** Remove the shrimp from the air fryer and let them cool slightly. Serve with the mango salsa on the side or spooned over the shrimp.
7. **Serve immediately:** Enjoy as a main dish or appetizer.

Servings: 4 | **Prep time:** 15 minutes | **Cooking time:** 8 minutes

Nutritional info: Calories: 250, Protein: 22g, Carbs: 20g, Fat: 10g

Quick tips:

- **Crispier Shrimp:** For extra crispy shrimp, toast the coconut-panko mixture in a dry skillet for a few minutes before coating the shrimp.
- **Mango Selection:** Choose a ripe mango for the salsa to ensure sweetness and balance with the lime.

Air Fryer Crispy Soft-Shell Crab

Air Fryer Crispy Soft-Shell Crab is a delicacy that combines the tender, juicy meat of soft-shell crab with a perfectly crispy coating. This dish is easy to prepare and offers a gourmet experience right from your kitchen, making it ideal for a special occasion or a seafood feast.

Tools needed:

Air fryer
Mixing bowls
Basting brush
Knife and cutting board
Tongs

Ingredients:

- 4 soft-shell crabs, cleaned and patted dry
- 1/2 cup flour
- 1/2 cup cornmeal
- 1 tsp Old Bay seasoning
- 1/2 tsp smoked paprika
- 1/4 tsp cayenne pepper (optional, for heat)
- 1/2 tsp salt
- 2 large eggs, beaten
- Olive oil spray
- Lemon wedges for serving
- Fresh herbs for garnish (optional)

Directions:

1. **Prepare the Coating:** In a mixing bowl, combine the flour, cornmeal, Old Bay seasoning, smoked paprika, cayenne pepper (if using), and salt. In a separate bowl, beat the eggs.
2. **Coat the Crabs:** Dredge each soft-shell crab in the flour-cornmeal mixture, then dip it into the beaten eggs, and finally coat it again in the flour-cornmeal mixture, pressing lightly to adhere.
3. **Preheat the Air Fryer:** Preheat your air fryer to 375°F (190°C).
4. **Cook the Crabs:** Arrange the coated crabs in the air fryer basket in a single layer. Lightly spray with olive oil. Cook at 375°F for 8-10 minutes, turning halfway through, until the crabs are golden brown and crispy.
5. **Serve:** Remove the crabs from the air fryer and let them rest for a minute. Serve with lemon wedges and garnish with fresh herbs if desired.
6. **Serve immediately:** Pair with a simple salad or coleslaw for a complete meal.

Servings: 4
Prep time: 15 minutes
Cooking time: 10 minutes

Nutritional info:
Calories: 300
Protein: 20g
Carbs: 25g
Fat: 12g

Quick tips:

- **Handling Crabs:** Be gentle when coating the soft-shell crabs to avoid breaking the delicate shells.
- **Extra Flavor:** Add a squeeze of fresh lemon juice over the crabs just before serving for a bright, fresh flavor.
- **Serving Suggestion:** These crabs pair wonderfully with a crisp white wine or a light, citrusy beer.

Air Fryer Blackened Catfish with Remoulade

Air Fryer Blackened Catfish is a delicious and bold dish that features catfish fillets coated in a spicy blackened seasoning. The air fryer gives the fish a perfect crispy crust while keeping the inside moist and tender.

Tools needed:

Air fryer
Mixing bowl
Basting brush
Knife and cutting board
Small bowl

Ingredients:
4 catfish fillets
2 tbsp olive oil
2 tbsp blackened seasoning (store-bought or homemade, see below)
Lemon wedges for serving
Fresh parsley for garnish (optional)
For the Remoulade:
1/2 cup mayonnaise
1 tbsp Dijon mustard
1 tbsp capers, finely chopped
1 tbsp pickles, finely chopped
1 tsp hot sauce
1 tsp Worcestershire sauce
1 tsp lemon juice
1 tsp smoked paprika
1 clove garlic, minced
Salt and pepper to taste

Directions:
For the Blackened Seasoning (if making homemade):
1 tbsp smoked paprika
1 tsp garlic powder
1 tsp onion powder
1 tsp dried thyme
1 tsp dried oregano
1 tsp cayenne pepper (optional, for heat)
1/2 tsp salt
1/2 tsp ground black pepper
Prepare the Blackened Seasoning (if using homemade): In a small bowl, mix together the smoked paprika, garlic powder, onion powder, thyme, oregano, cayenne pepper, salt, and black pepper. Set aside.
Season the Catfish: Pat the catfish fillets dry with paper towels. Brush both sides of the fillets with olive oil. Generously coat the fillets with the blackened seasoning, pressing it into the fish to ensure it adheres well.
Preheat the Air Fryer: Preheat your air fryer to 375°F (190°C).
Cook the Catfish: Place the seasoned catfish fillets in the air fryer basket in a single layer. Cook at 375°F for 10-12 minutes, flipping halfway through, until the fish is cooked through and has a crispy, blackened crust.
Make the Remoulade: While the catfish is cooking, prepare the remoulade sauce. In a small bowl, mix together the mayonnaise, Dijon mustard, capers, pickles, hot sauce, Worcestershire sauce, lemon juice, smoked paprika, minced garlic, salt, and pepper. Stir until well combined and smooth.
Serve: Remove the catfish from the air fryer and let it rest for a minute. Serve the fish with the remoulade sauce on the side, garnished with fresh parsley and lemon wedges if desired.

Servings: 4 | **Prep time:** 10 minutes | **Cooking time:** 12 minutes

Nutritional info: Calories: 350, Protein: 30g, Carbs: 4g, Fat: 24g

Quick tips:

- **Even Cooking:** Make sure the catfish fillets are of similar thickness to ensure even cooking.
- **Adjusting Spice:** For a milder version, reduce the amount of cayenne pepper in the blackened seasoning.

AIRFRYER LAMB RECIPES

Lamb Ribs with Pomegranate Molasses Glaze

These Air Fryer Lamb Ribs are tender, juicy, and packed with flavor. The ribs are first seasoned and cooked to perfection in the air fryer, then finished with a sticky and tangy pomegranate molasses glaze. This dish is perfect for a special dinner or when you want to impress your guests.

Tools needed:

Air fryer
Mixing bowl
Basting brush
Knife and cutting board
Small saucepan

Ingredients:

- 1.5 lbs lamb ribs, cut into individual ribs
- 1 tsp ground cumin
- 1 tsp ground coriander
- 1/2 tsp ground cinnamon
- 1/2 tsp garlic powder
- 1/2 tsp smoked paprika
- Salt and pepper to taste
- 1 tbsp olive oil

For the Pomegranate Molasses Glaze:

- 1/4 cup pomegranate molasses
- 2 tbsp honey
- 1 tbsp soy sauce
- 1 tsp lemon juice
- 1/4 tsp ground black pepper

Directions:

Prepare the Spice Rub: In a mixing bowl, combine the ground cumin, coriander, cinnamon, garlic powder, smoked paprika, salt, and pepper. Rub the lamb ribs with olive oil, then coat them evenly with the spice mixture.

Preheat the Air Fryer: Preheat your air fryer to 375°F (190°C).

Cook the Lamb Ribs: Arrange the lamb ribs in a single layer in the air fryer basket. Cook at 375°F for 20-25 minutes, turning halfway through, until the ribs are browned and tender.

Make the Pomegranate Molasses Glaze: While the ribs are cooking, combine pomegranate molasses, honey, soy sauce, lemon juice, and ground black pepper in a small saucepan. Heat over medium heat, stirring occasionally, until the glaze thickens slightly, about 5 minutes. Remove from heat.

Glaze the Ribs: During the last 5 minutes of cooking, brush the lamb ribs generously with the pomegranate molasses glaze. Continue cooking until the glaze is sticky and caramelized.

Serve: Remove the ribs from the air fryer and let them rest for a few minutes. Serve with additional glaze on the side if desired.

Servings: 4 | **Prep time:** 10 minutes | **Cooking time:** 25 minutes
Nutritional info: Calories: 400, Protein: 20g, Carbs: 18g, Fat: 28g

Quick tips:

- **Pomegranate Molasses Substitute:** If you can't find pomegranate molasses, you can make a quick substitute by reducing pomegranate juice with sugar and lemon juice until syrupy.
- **Serving Suggestion:** Garnish with fresh pomegranate seeds and chopped parsley for added color and flavor.
- **Resting:** Letting the ribs rest after cooking allows the juices to redistribute, making them more tender.

Lamb Kofta with Minted Yogurt and Pine Nuts

Lamb Kofta is a delicious Middle Eastern dish made from ground lamb, spices, and herbs, shaped into meatballs or patties.

Tools needed:

Air fryer
Mixing bowl
Knife and cutting board
Skewers (optional)

Ingredients:

- 1 lb ground lamb
- 1 small onion, finely chopped
- 2 cloves garlic, minced
- 2 tbsp fresh parsley, chopped
- 1 tbsp fresh mint, chopped
- 1 tsp ground cumin
- 1 tsp ground coriander
- 1/2 tsp ground cinnamon
- 1/2 tsp paprika
- 1/4 tsp cayenne pepper (optional)
- Salt and pepper to taste
- 1 tbsp olive oil

For the Minted Yogurt:

- 1/2 cup plain Greek yogurt
- 1 tbsp fresh mint, finely chopped
- 1 tsp lemon juice
- Salt and pepper to taste

For Garnish:

- 2 tbsp pine nuts, toasted
- Fresh mint leaves

Directions:

1. **Prepare the Kofta Mixture:** In a mixing bowl, combine the ground lamb, chopped onion, minced garlic, parsley, mint, cumin, coriander, cinnamon, paprika, cayenne pepper (if using), salt, and pepper. Mix well until all ingredients are fully incorporated.
2. **Shape the Koftas:** Divide the mixture into equal portions and shape them into oval patties or meatballs. If using skewers, you can thread the patties onto the skewers.
3. **Preheat the Air Fryer:** Preheat your air fryer to 375°F (190°C).
4. **Cook the Koftas:** Brush the koftas with olive oil and place them in the air fryer basket in a single layer. Cook at 375°F for 10-12 minutes, turning halfway through, until the koftas are browned and cooked through.
5. **Make the Minted Yogurt:** While the koftas are cooking, mix the Greek yogurt, chopped mint, lemon juice, salt, and pepper in a small bowl. Stir until well combined.
6. **Serve:** Remove the koftas from the air fryer and serve with minted yogurt on the side. Garnish with toasted pine nuts and fresh mint leaves.

Servings: 4 | **Prep time:** 15 minutes | **Cooking time:** 12 minutes

Nutritional info: Calories: 320, Protein: 22g, Carbs: 4g, Fat: 24g

Quick tips:

- **Make Ahead:** The kofta mixture can be prepared ahead of time and stored in the refrigerator for up to 24 hours before cooking.
- **Yogurt Sauce:** The minted yogurt can be made a few hours in advance and kept in the refrigerator to allow the flavors to meld.

Merguez Sausages with Harissa Mayo

Merguez sausages are spicy North African lamb sausages packed with flavor. This air fryer version ensures the sausages are cooked to perfection, with a crispy exterior and juicy interior. They are served with a spicy harissa mayo, making them perfect for a flavorful appetizer or main course.

Tools needed:

Air fryer
Mixing bowl
Knife and cutting board
Small bowl

Ingredients:

- 1 lb merguez sausages
- 1 tbsp olive oil

For the Harissa Mayo:

- 1/2 cup mayonnaise
- 1 tbsp harissa paste (adjust to taste)
- 1 tsp lemon juice
- 1 clove garlic, minced
- Salt and pepper to taste

Directions:

1. **Preheat the Air Fryer:** Preheat your air fryer to 375°F (190°C).
2. **Cook the Merguez Sausages:** Lightly brush the sausages with olive oil and place them in the air fryer basket. Cook at 375°F for 10-12 minutes, turning halfway through, until the sausages are browned and cooked through.
3. **Make the Harissa Mayo:** While the sausages are cooking, mix the mayonnaise, harissa paste, lemon juice, minced garlic, salt, and pepper in a small bowl. Stir until well combined and smooth.
4. **Serve:** Remove the sausages from the air fryer and let them rest for a minute. Serve with the harissa mayo on the side.
5. **Serve immediately:** Enjoy the merguez sausages as an appetizer or pair with a side of couscous or roasted vegetables for a complete meal.

Servings: 4
Prep time: 5 minutes
Cooking time: 12 minutes

Nutritional info:
Calories: 350
Protein: 18g
Carbs: 2g
Fat: 30g

Quick tips:

- **Adjusting Spice:** Adjust the amount of harissa in the mayo according to your spice preference.
- **Serving Suggestion:** Serve with grilled flatbread and a side of olives for a Mediterranean-inspired meal.
- **Leftover Use:** Leftover sausages can be sliced and added to salads or grain bowls for an easy lunch the next day.

Persian Lamb Shanks with Saffron and Prunes

Persian Lamb Shanks with Saffron and Prunes is a luxurious, slow-cooked dish that combines tender lamb with the rich flavors of saffron, prunes, and spices.

Tools needed:

Large pot or Dutch oven
Air fryer
Mixing bowl
Small bowl for saffron infusion
Knife and cutting board

Ingredients:

- 2 lamb shanks
- 1 large onion, finely chopped
- 4 cloves garlic, minced
- 1 tsp ground cinnamon
- 1 tsp ground cumin
- 1/2 tsp ground turmeric
- 1/4 tsp ground black pepper
- 1/2 cup prunes, pitted
- 1/2 tsp saffron threads, steeped in 2 tbsp warm water
- 1 cup beef or lamb broth
- 1/2 cup water
- 2 tbsp olive oil
- Salt to taste
- Fresh cilantro or parsley for garnish (optional)

Directions:

1. **Prepare the Lamb Shanks:** Season the lamb shanks with salt, pepper, cinnamon, cumin, and turmeric. In a large pot or Dutch oven, heat the olive oil over medium-high heat. Brown the lamb shanks on all sides, about 10 minutes total. Remove and set aside.
2. **Sauté the Onions and Garlic:** In the same pot, add the chopped onion and garlic. Cook until softened and golden brown, about 5-7 minutes.
3. **Add the Prunes and Broth:** Add the prunes, saffron water, broth, and water to the pot. Stir to combine. Return the lamb shanks to the pot, making sure they are partially submerged in the liquid.
4. **Slow Cook the Lamb Shanks:** Cover the pot and reduce the heat to low. Simmer for 2-2.5 hours, turning the shanks occasionally, until the meat is tender and falling off the bone.
5. **Finish in the Air Fryer (Optional):** For a crispier exterior, transfer the lamb shanks to the air fryer basket. Air fry at 400°F (200°C) for 5-7 minutes, until the outside is slightly crispy.
6. **Serve:** Remove the lamb shanks from the pot or air fryer and place them on a serving dish. Drizzle the saffron-prune sauce over the shanks. Garnish with fresh cilantro or parsley if desired.

Servings: 2 | **Prep time:** 20 minutes | **Cooking time:** 2.5 hours
Nutritional info: Calories: 500, Protein: 35g, Carbs: 25g, Fat: 28g

Quick tips:

- **Saffron Infusion:** For the best saffron flavor, steep the saffron threads in warm water for at least 10 minutes before adding them to the dish.
- **Make Ahead:** This dish can be made a day ahead and reheated; the flavors will deepen as it sits.

Air Fryer Lamb Kebabs with Cumin and Sumac

These Air Fryer Lamb Kebabs are seasoned with cumin, sumac, and fresh herbs, offering a Middle Eastern-inspired flavor that's both aromatic and savory. The air fryer ensures the kebabs are cooked evenly with a slightly charred exterior, making them a perfect choice for a quick and delicious meal.

Tools needed:

Air fryer
Skewers (metal or soaked wooden skewers)
Mixing bowl
Knife and cutting board

Ingredients:

- 1 lb ground lamb
- 1 small onion, finely grated
- 2 cloves garlic, minced
- 2 tbsp fresh parsley, chopped
- 1 tbsp ground cumin
- 1 tbsp ground sumac
- 1 tsp ground coriander
- 1/2 tsp ground cinnamon
- 1/4 tsp cayenne pepper (optional)
- Salt and pepper to taste
- 1 tbsp olive oil
- Lemon wedges for serving
- Fresh mint leaves for garnish (optional)

Directions:

1. **Prepare the Kebab Mixture:** In a mixing bowl, combine the ground lamb, grated onion, minced garlic, parsley, cumin, sumac, coriander, cinnamon, cayenne pepper (if using), salt, and pepper. Mix until all ingredients are fully incorporated.
2. **Shape the Kebabs:** Divide the mixture into equal portions and shape them into long, oval kebabs. If using skewers, thread the kebabs onto the skewers, pressing them tightly around the skewer.
3. **Preheat the Air Fryer:** Preheat your air fryer to 375°F (190°C).
4. **Cook the Kebabs:** Lightly brush the kebabs with olive oil and place them in the air fryer basket. Cook at 375°F for 10-12 minutes, turning halfway through, until the kebabs are browned and cooked through.
5. **Serve:** Remove the kebabs from the air fryer and let them rest for a minute. Serve with lemon wedges and garnish with fresh mint leaves if desired.
6. **Serve immediately:** Enjoy with warm pita bread, hummus, and a fresh salad.

Servings: 4
Prep time: 15 minutes
Cooking time: 12 minutes

Nutritional info:
Calories: 300
Protein: 22g
Carbs: 4g
Fat: 22g

Quick tips:

- **Sumac Flavor:** Sumac adds a tangy, lemony flavor to the kebabs; adjust the amount to your taste.
- **Serving Suggestion:** Pair with a simple yogurt dip flavored with garlic and lemon for a cooling contrast.
- **Grill Option:** These kebabs can also be grilled for a smoky flavor if desired.

Lamb-Stuffed Grape Leaves with Lemon Dill Sauce

Lamb-Stuffed Grape Leaves are a Mediterranean classic that combines tender grape leaves with a flavorful lamb and rice filling. The addition of a tangy lemon dill sauce brings freshness and brightness to the dish, making it perfect for appetizers or a main course.

Tools needed:

Air fryer
Large pot for boiling grape leaves
Mixing bowl
Knife and cutting board
Small saucepan for sauce

Ingredients:

- 1 jar grape leaves, rinsed and drained
- 1/2 lb ground lamb
- 1/2 cup uncooked rice (short-grain works best)
- 1 small onion, finely chopped
- 2 cloves garlic, minced
- 1 tbsp fresh dill, chopped
- 1 tbsp fresh parsley, chopped
- 1 tsp ground cumin
- 1 tsp ground coriander
- 1/2 tsp ground cinnamon
- Salt and pepper to taste
- 2 tbsp olive oil
- 1/4 cup water or chicken broth

For the Lemon Dill Sauce:

- 1/2 cup Greek yogurt
- 1 tbsp fresh dill, chopped
- 1 tbsp lemon juice
- 1 tsp lemon zest
- Salt and pepper to taste

Directions:

Prepare the Filling: In a mixing bowl, combine the ground lamb, uncooked rice, chopped onion, minced garlic, dill, parsley, cumin, coriander, cinnamon, salt, and pepper. Mix well until all ingredients are fully incorporated.

Stuff the Grape Leaves: Lay each grape leaf shiny side down on a flat surface. Place about 1 tablespoon of the filling in the center of each leaf. Fold the sides over the filling and roll tightly into a cylinder. Repeat with the remaining leaves and filling.

Cook the Grape Leaves: Preheat your air fryer to 350°F (175°C). Lightly brush the stuffed grape leaves with olive oil and place them in the air fryer basket in a single layer. Cook at 350°F for 10-12 minutes, turning halfway through, until the grape leaves are slightly crispy on the outside and the filling is cooked through.

Make the Lemon Dill Sauce: While the grape leaves are cooking, prepare the sauce by mixing the Greek yogurt, chopped dill, lemon juice, lemon zest, salt, and pepper in a small bowl. Stir until well combined.

Serve: Remove the grape leaves from the air fryer and let them cool slightly. Serve with the lemon dill sauce on the side.

Serve immediately: Enjoy as an appetizer or pair with a Mediterranean salad for a complete meal.

Servings: 4 | **Prep time:** 25 minutes | **Cooking time:** 12 minutes

Nutritional info: Calories: 250, Protein: 12g, Carbs: 20g, Fat: 14g

Quick tips:

- **Grape Leaves:** If using fresh grape leaves, blanch them in boiling water for 2-3 minutes to soften before stuffing.
- **Make Ahead:** These grape leaves can be prepared ahead of time and reheated in the air fryer just before serving.

Lamb Neck Fillets with Garlic and Rosemary

Air Fryer Lamb Neck Fillets with Garlic and Rosemary is a simple yet flavorful dish that highlights the rich taste of lamb neck, a tender cut that becomes even more delicious when infused with the classic combination of garlic and rosemary. The air fryer ensures the fillets are perfectly seared on the outside while remaining juicy and tender on the inside.

Tools needed:

Air fryer
Mixing bowl
Basting brush
Knife and cutting board

Ingredients:

- 4 lamb neck fillets (about 1 inch thick)
- 3 cloves garlic, minced
- 2 tbsp fresh rosemary, chopped
- 2 tbsp olive oil
- Salt and pepper to taste
- Lemon wedges for serving (optional)

Directions:

1. **Prepare the Marinade:** In a mixing bowl, combine the minced garlic, chopped rosemary, olive oil, salt, and pepper. Mix well to form a marinade.
2. **Marinate the Lamb Fillets:** Rub the lamb neck fillets with the marinade, ensuring they are evenly coated. Let them marinate for at least 30 minutes, preferably 2 hours, in the refrigerator.
3. **Preheat the Air Fryer:** Preheat your air fryer to 375°F (190°C).
4. **Cook the Lamb Fillets:** Place the marinated lamb neck fillets in the air fryer basket in a single layer. Cook at 375°F for 12-15 minutes, turning halfway through, until the lamb is browned and cooked to your desired level of doneness (internal temperature should reach 145°F for medium-rare).
5. **Rest and Serve:** Remove the lamb fillets from the air fryer and let them rest for 5 minutes. This allows the juices to redistribute, making the meat more tender.
6. **Serve:** Slice the lamb fillets and serve with lemon wedges on the side for a fresh citrus finish.
7. **Serve immediately:** Pair with roasted vegetables or a fresh salad for a complete meal.

Servings: 4
Prep time: 10 minutes (plus marinating time)
Cooking time: 15 minutes

Nutritional info:
Calories: 350
Protein: 28g
Carbs: 2g
Fat: 24g

Quick tips:

- **Marinating Time:** For more intense flavor, marinate the lamb fillets overnight.
- **Even Cooking:** Make sure the fillets are of similar thickness for even cooking.
- **Serving Suggestion:** Complement with a side of garlic mashed potatoes or a grain salad for a hearty meal.

Air Fryer Moroccan Lamb Tagine Skewers

These Air Fryer Moroccan Lamb Tagine Skewers bring the rich, aromatic flavors of a traditional Moroccan tagine into a convenient, grill-like format. The lamb is marinated in a blend of spices and herbs, then skewered and air-fried to juicy perfection. These skewers are perfect for a flavorful and exotic meal.

Tools needed:

Air fryer
Skewers (metal or soaked wooden skewers)
Mixing bowl
Knife and cutting board

Ingredients:

- 1 lb lamb shoulder or leg, cut into 1-inch cubes
- 1 small onion, finely chopped
- 2 cloves garlic, minced
- 1 tbsp fresh cilantro, chopped
- 1 tbsp fresh parsley, chopped
- 1 tsp ground cumin
- 1 tsp ground coriander
- 1 tsp ground cinnamon
- 1/2 tsp ground turmeric
- 1/4 tsp ground ginger
- 1/4 tsp cayenne pepper (optional)
- 1 tbsp olive oil
- Salt and pepper to taste
- Lemon wedges for serving
- Fresh mint leaves for garnish (optional)

Directions:

1. **Prepare the Marinade:** In a mixing bowl, combine the chopped onion, minced garlic, cilantro, parsley, cumin, coriander, cinnamon, turmeric, ginger, cayenne pepper (if using), olive oil, salt, and pepper. Mix well.
2. **Marinate the Lamb:** Add the lamb cubes to the marinade, tossing to coat evenly. Cover and refrigerate for at least 1 hour, preferably overnight, to allow the flavors to meld.
3. **Preheat the Air Fryer:** Preheat your air fryer to 375°F (190°C).
4. **Assemble the Skewers:** Thread the marinated lamb cubes onto skewers, leaving a little space between each piece for even cooking.
5. **Cook the Skewers:** Place the skewers in the air fryer basket in a single layer. Cook at 375°F for 10-12 minutes, turning halfway through, until the lamb is browned and cooked through.
6. **Serve:** Remove the skewers from the air fryer and let them rest for a minute. Serve with lemon wedges and garnish with fresh mint leaves if desired.
7. **Serve immediately:** Pair with couscous, a fresh salad, or roasted vegetables for a complete meal.

Servings: 4
Prep time: 15 minutes (plus marinating time)
Cooking time: 12 minutes

Nutritional info: Calories: 320, Protein: 25g, Carbs: 4g, Fat: 22g

Quick tips:

- **Marinating Time:** The longer the lamb marinates, the more flavorful it will be. Overnight marination is ideal.
- **Grill Option:** These skewers can also be cooked on a grill for a smoky flavor if desired.
- **Serving Suggestion:** Serve with a side of harissa or yogurt sauce for dipping.

Crispy Okra with Tamarind Chutney

Air Fryer Crispy Okra is a delicious and healthier twist on the classic fried okra, with a light and crunchy texture. Paired with a tangy tamarind chutney, this dish makes for a perfect appetizer or snack with a burst of flavors.

Tools needed:

Air fryer
Mixing bowl
Knife and cutting board
Small saucepan for chutney

Ingredients:

- 1 lb fresh okra, trimmed and cut lengthwise into halves
- 2 tbsp chickpea flour (besan)
- 1 tbsp rice flour
- 1 tsp ground cumin
- 1 tsp ground coriander
- 1/2 tsp turmeric powder
- 1/4 tsp cayenne pepper (optional)
- 1 tbsp olive oil
- Salt to taste

For the Tamarind Chutney:

- 1/4 cup tamarind paste
- 1/4 cup water
- 2 tbsp jaggery or brown sugar
- 1/2 tsp ground cumin
- 1/2 tsp ground coriander
- 1/4 tsp cayenne pepper (optional)
- Salt to taste

Directions:

1. **Prepare the Okra:** In a mixing bowl, combine the chickpea flour, rice flour, cumin, coriander, turmeric, cayenne pepper (if using), and salt. Toss the okra in the spice mixture, ensuring each piece is evenly coated. Drizzle with olive oil and toss again.
2. **Preheat the Air Fryer:** Preheat your air fryer to 375°F (190°C).
3. **Cook the Okra:** Place the coated okra in the air fryer basket in a single layer. Cook at 375°F for 10-12 minutes, shaking the basket halfway through, until the okra is crispy and golden brown.
4. **Make the Tamarind Chutney:** While the okra is cooking, combine tamarind paste, water, jaggery (or brown sugar), cumin, coriander, cayenne pepper, and salt in a small saucepan. Bring to a simmer over medium heat, stirring until the chutney thickens, about 5 minutes. Remove from heat and let cool.
5. **Serve:** Remove the crispy okra from the air fryer and transfer to a serving plate. Serve with tamarind chutney on the side for dipping.

Servings: 4 | **Prep time:** 10 minutes | **Cooking time:** 12 minutes

Nutritional info: Calories: 150, Protein: 3g, Carbs: 20g, Fat: 7g

Quick tips:

- **Avoid Sogginess:** Pat the okra dry thoroughly before coating to avoid sogginess.
- **Chutney Storage:** Tamarind chutney can be made ahead of time and stored in the refrigerator for up to a week.

Air Fryer Polenta Fries with Gorgonzola Dip

Air Fryer Polenta Fries are a crispy, golden treat with a creamy interior, making them a delightful alternative to regular fries. Paired with a rich and tangy Gorgonzola dip, these fries are perfect as an appetizer or side dish for a sophisticated yet comforting experience.

Tools needed:

Air fryer
Baking dish
Mixing bowl
Knife and cutting board
Small saucepan for dip

Ingredients:

- 1 cup instant polenta
- 3 cups water or vegetable broth
- 1/2 cup grated Parmesan cheese
- 1 tbsp butter
- 1/2 tsp salt
- 1/4 tsp black pepper
- 1 tbsp olive oil

For the Gorgonzola Dip:

- 1/2 cup Gorgonzola cheese, crumbled
- 1/4 cup heavy cream
- 1 tbsp sour cream
- 1 tsp lemon juice
- Freshly ground black pepper to taste

Directions:

1. **Prepare the Polenta:** In a saucepan, bring water or vegetable broth to a boil. Gradually whisk in the polenta, stirring constantly to prevent lumps. Cook until thickened, about 5 minutes. Remove from heat and stir in the Parmesan cheese, butter, salt, and pepper.
2. **Set the Polenta:** Pour the polenta into a lightly greased baking dish and spread it evenly. Let it cool completely until firm, about 1 hour. Once firm, cut the polenta into fry-shaped strips.
3. **Preheat the Air Fryer:** Preheat your air fryer to 400°F (200°C).
4. **Cook the Polenta Fries:** Lightly brush the polenta fries with olive oil. Place them in the air fryer basket in a single layer. Cook at 400°F for 10-12 minutes, turning halfway through, until the fries are golden and crispy.
5. **Make the Gorgonzola Dip:** While the fries are cooking, prepare the dip by combining Gorgonzola cheese, heavy cream, sour cream, lemon juice, and black pepper in a small saucepan. Heat over low heat, stirring until the cheese is melted and the dip is smooth.
6. **Serve:** Remove the polenta fries from the air fryer and transfer to a serving plate. Serve with the warm Gorgonzola dip on the side.
7. **Serve immediately:** Enjoy as an appetizer or side dish.

Servings: 4 | **Prep time:** 15 minutes (plus cooling time) | **Cooking time:** 12 minutes

Nutritional info: Calories: 250, Protein: 8g, Carbs: 35g, Fat: 10g

Quick tips:

- **Crispier Fries:** For extra crispiness, allow the polenta fries to cool slightly before air frying.
- **Dip Variations:** Add a bit of crushed garlic or fresh herbs to the Gorgonzola dip for added flavor.
- **Serving Suggestion:** Pair with a glass of white wine or a light beer to complement the creamy dip.

Miso-Roasted Japanese Eggplant with Sesame Seeds

Miso-Roasted Japanese Eggplant is a savory and umami-rich dish that highlights the tender and slightly sweet nature of Japanese eggplant. The miso glaze adds depth of flavor, while the sesame seeds provide a nutty crunch. This dish is a perfect side or light vegetarian main course.

Tools needed:

Air fryer
Mixing bowl
Basting brush
Knife and cutting board

Ingredients:

- 2 Japanese eggplants, halved lengthwise
- 2 tbsp white miso paste
- 1 tbsp mirin (Japanese sweet rice wine)
- 1 tbsp soy sauce
- 1 tbsp sesame oil
- 1 tsp rice vinegar
- 1 tbsp honey or maple syrup
- 1 tbsp sesame seeds, toasted
- Chopped green onions for garnish (optional)

Directions:

1. **Prepare the Miso Glaze:** In a mixing bowl, combine miso paste, mirin, soy sauce, sesame oil, rice vinegar, and honey (or maple syrup). Mix until smooth.
2. **Brush the Eggplant:** Score the flesh of the eggplant halves in a crosshatch pattern. Brush the miso glaze generously over the cut sides of the eggplant.
3. **Preheat the Air Fryer:** Preheat your air fryer to 375°F (190°C).
4. **Cook the Eggplant:** Place the glazed eggplant halves in the air fryer basket, cut side up. Cook at 375°F for 15-18 minutes, or until the eggplant is tender and caramelized.
5. **Serve:** Remove the eggplant from the air fryer and transfer to a serving plate. Sprinkle with toasted sesame seeds and garnish with chopped green onions if desired.
6. **Serve immediately:** Enjoy as a side dish or light main course.

Servings: 4
Prep time: 10 minutes
Cooking time: 18 minutes

Nutritional info:
Calories: 120
Protein: 2g
Carbs: 14g
Fat: 7g

Quick tips:

- **Even Cooking:** Ensure the eggplants are of similar size for even cooking.
- **Glaze Variations:** For a spicy kick, add a small amount of chili paste to the miso glaze.
- **Serving Suggestion:** Pair with steamed rice or quinoa to soak up the delicious miso glaze.

Air Fryer Cauliflower Steaks with Romesco Sauce

Air Fryer Cauliflower Steaks with Romesco Sauce is a vibrant and flavorful dish that showcases the versatility of cauliflower. The cauliflower steaks are air-fried to a perfect golden brown, then topped with a rich and smoky Romesco sauce made from roasted red peppers, almonds, and garlic.

Tools needed:

Air fryer
Knife and cutting board
Food processor or blender
Basting brush

Ingredients:

For the Cauliflower Steaks:

- 1 large head of cauliflower
- 2 tbsp olive oil
- 1 tsp smoked paprika
- 1/2 tsp garlic powder
- 1/2 tsp onion powder
- Salt and pepper to taste

For the Romesco Sauce:

- 1/2 cup roasted red peppers, drained
- 1/4 cup toasted almonds
- 2 cloves garlic
- 1 tbsp tomato paste
- 1 tbsp red wine vinegar
- 1/2 tsp smoked paprika
- 1/4 cup olive oil
- Salt and pepper to taste

Directions:

1. **Prepare the Cauliflower Steaks:** Remove the leaves from the cauliflower and trim the stem. Cut the cauliflower into 1-inch thick steaks, slicing from the top to the base. Brush both sides of each steak with olive oil and season with smoked paprika, garlic powder, onion powder, salt, and pepper.
2. **Preheat the Air Fryer:** Preheat your air fryer to 375°F (190°C).
3. **Cook the Cauliflower Steaks:** Place the cauliflower steaks in the air fryer basket in a single layer. Cook at 375°F for 12-15 minutes, flipping halfway through, until the cauliflower is tender and golden brown.
4. **Make the Romesco Sauce:** While the cauliflower is cooking, prepare the Romesco sauce. In a food processor or blender, combine roasted red peppers, toasted almonds, garlic, tomato paste, red wine vinegar, smoked paprika, salt, and pepper. Blend until smooth, then slowly drizzle in the olive oil while continuing to blend until the sauce is emulsified.
5. **Serve:** Remove the cauliflower steaks from the air fryer and transfer to a serving plate. Spoon the Romesco sauce over the steaks.
6. **Serve immediately:** Enjoy as a main dish or a flavorful side.

Servings: 4 | **Prep time:** 15 minutes | **Cooking time:** 15 minutes

Nutritional info: Calories: 200, Protein: 4g, Carbs: 12g, Fat: 16g

Quick tips:

- **Even Cooking:** Make sure the cauliflower steaks are of similar thickness for even cooking.
- **Romesco Sauce:** The Romesco sauce can be made ahead of time and stored in the refrigerator for up to 3 days.

Stuffed Peppers with Farro, Walnuts, and Feta

Stuffed Peppers with Farro, Walnuts, and Feta is a wholesome and satisfying dish filled with nutty farro, crunchy walnuts, and creamy feta cheese. These peppers are air-fried to perfection, making them a quick and easy yet impressive vegetarian meal.

Tools needed:

Air fryer
Mixing bowl
Knife and cutting board
Saucepan for cooking farro

Ingredients:

- 4 bell peppers, halved and seeds removed
- 1 cup cooked farro
- 1/2 cup walnuts, toasted and chopped
- 1/2 cup crumbled feta cheese
- 1/4 cup sun-dried tomatoes, chopped
- 2 tbsp fresh parsley, chopped
- 2 cloves garlic, minced
- 1 tbsp olive oil
- 1 tsp dried oregano
- Salt and pepper to taste

Directions:

1. **Prepare the Filling:** In a mixing bowl, combine the cooked farro, chopped walnuts, crumbled feta, sun-dried tomatoes, parsley, minced garlic, olive oil, oregano, salt, and pepper. Mix until well combined.
2. **Stuff the Peppers:** Spoon the farro mixture into the halved bell peppers, packing it down slightly.
3. **Preheat the Air Fryer:** Preheat your air fryer to 375°F (190°C).
4. **Cook the Stuffed Peppers:** Place the stuffed peppers in the air fryer basket in a single layer. Cook at 375°F for 12-15 minutes, until the peppers are tender and the filling is heated through.
5. **Serve:** Remove the stuffed peppers from the air fryer and let them cool slightly before serving.
6. **Serve immediately:** Enjoy as a main dish or a hearty side.

Servings: 4
Prep time: 15 minutes
Cooking time: 15 minutes

Nutritional info:
Calories: 250
Protein: 8g
Carbs: 28g
Fat: 12g

Quick tips:

- **Pepper Variety:** Use a mix of colorful bell peppers for a visually appealing dish.
- **Make Ahead:** The filling can be prepared ahead of time and refrigerated until ready to stuff and cook the peppers.
- **Serving Suggestion:** Pair with a side of tzatziki or a Greek salad for a Mediterranean-inspired meal.

Crispy Artichoke Hearts with Lemon Herb Dip

Air Fryer Crispy Artichoke Hearts are a delightful appetizer or snack with a golden, crunchy exterior and a tender interior. Paired with a tangy lemon herb dip, these artichoke hearts are both flavorful and easy to make, offering a gourmet experience in every bite.

Tools needed:

Air fryer
Mixing bowls
Knife and cutting board
Small bowl for dip

Ingredients:

For the Artichoke Hearts:

- 1 can (14 oz) artichoke hearts, drained and patted dry
- 1/2 cup panko breadcrumbs
- 1/4 cup grated Parmesan cheese
- 1 tsp garlic powder
- 1/2 tsp dried oregano
- 1/4 tsp salt
- 1/4 tsp black pepper
- 1 egg, beaten
- Olive oil spray

For the Lemon Herb Dip:

- 1/2 cup Greek yogurt or sour cream
- 1 tbsp lemon juice
- 1 tsp lemon zest
- 1 tbsp fresh parsley, chopped
- 1 tbsp fresh dill, chopped
- 1 clove garlic, minced
- Salt and pepper to taste

Directions:

1. **Prepare the Artichoke Hearts:** In a mixing bowl, combine panko breadcrumbs, Parmesan cheese, garlic powder, oregano, salt, and pepper. Dip each artichoke heart into the beaten egg, then coat with the breadcrumb mixture, pressing lightly to adhere.
2. **Preheat the Air Fryer:** Preheat your air fryer to 375°F (190°C).
3. **Cook the Artichoke Hearts:** Place the breaded artichoke hearts in the air fryer basket in a single layer. Lightly spray with olive oil. Cook at 375°F for 10-12 minutes, turning halfway through, until golden and crispy.
4. **Make the Lemon Herb Dip:** While the artichoke hearts are cooking, prepare the dip by combining Greek yogurt (or sour cream), lemon juice, lemon zest, parsley, dill, garlic, salt, and pepper in a small bowl. Stir until well mixed.
5. **Serve:** Remove the crispy artichoke hearts from the air fryer and transfer to a serving plate. Serve with the lemon herb dip on the side.
6. **Serve immediately:** Enjoy as an appetizer or snack.

Servings: 4 | **Prep time:** 10 minutes | **Cooking time:** 12 minutes

Nutritional info: Calories: 180, Protein: 6g, Carbs: 15g, Fat: 10g

Quick tips:

- **Crispier Texture:** Ensure the artichoke hearts are thoroughly patted dry before breading to achieve the crispiest texture.
- **Dip Variations:** Add a pinch of red pepper flakes to the dip for a spicy kick.

Crispy Air Fryer Tofu with Ginger-Soy Glaze

Crispy Air Fryer Tofu with Ginger-Soy Glaze is a flavorful and satisfying dish that turns tofu into a crispy, savory delight. The tofu is air-fried to perfection and then tossed in a sweet and spicy ginger-soy glaze, making it a delicious main or side dish.

Tools needed:

Air fryer
Mixing bowls
Knife and cutting board
Small saucepan for glaze

Ingredients:

For the Tofu:

- 1 block (14 oz) firm tofu, drained and pressed
- 2 tbsp cornstarch
- 1 tbsp olive oil
- 1/2 tsp garlic powder
- 1/2 tsp ground ginger
- Salt and pepper to taste

For the Ginger-Soy Glaze:

- 1/4 cup soy sauce
- 2 tbsp honey or maple syrup
- 1 tbsp rice vinegar
- 1 tbsp fresh ginger, grated
- 2 cloves garlic, minced
- 1 tsp sesame oil
- 1/2 tsp red pepper flakes (optional)
- 1 tsp cornstarch mixed with 1 tbsp water (slurry)

Directions:

1. **Prepare the Tofu:** Cut the pressed tofu into 1-inch cubes. In a mixing bowl, toss the tofu cubes with cornstarch, garlic powder, ground ginger, salt, and pepper until evenly coated.
2. **Preheat the Air Fryer:** Preheat your air fryer to 375°F (190°C).
3. **Cook the Tofu:** Place the tofu cubes in the air fryer basket in a single layer. Lightly spray with olive oil. Cook at 375°F for 12-15 minutes, shaking the basket halfway through, until the tofu is golden and crispy.
4. **Make the Ginger-Soy Glaze:** While the tofu is cooking, prepare the glaze. In a small saucepan, combine soy sauce, honey (or maple syrup), rice vinegar, grated ginger, minced garlic, sesame oil, and red pepper flakes (if using). Bring to a simmer over medium heat. Stir in the cornstarch slurry and cook for another 1-2 minutes until the sauce thickens.
5. **Toss the Tofu in Glaze:** Once the tofu is done, transfer it to a mixing bowl and toss with the ginger-soy glaze until evenly coated.

Servings: 4 | **Prep time:** 10 minutes | **Cooking time:** 15 minutes

Nutritional info: Calories: 200, Protein: 10g, Carbs: 12g, Fat: 12g

Quick tips:

- **Pressing Tofu:** Ensure the tofu is well-pressed to remove excess moisture for the crispiest texture.
- **Glaze Adjustments:** For a sweeter glaze, add more honey or maple syrup; for a spicier kick, increase the red pepper flakes.

Balsamic Glazed Brussels Sprouts

Air Fryer Balsamic Glazed Brussels Sprouts are a delicious and healthy side dish that combines the natural sweetness of Brussels sprouts with a tangy balsamic glaze. The air fryer gives the sprouts a crispy, caramelized exterior while keeping the inside tender.

Tools needed:

Air fryer
Mixing bowl
Small saucepan for glaze
Basting brush

Ingredients:

- 1 lb Brussels sprouts, trimmed and halved
- 2 tbsp olive oil
- Salt and pepper to taste

For the Balsamic Glaze:

- 1/4 cup balsamic vinegar
- 2 tbsp honey or maple syrup
- 1 clove garlic, minced
- 1/4 tsp salt
- 1/4 tsp black pepper

Directions:

1. **Prepare the Brussels Sprouts:** In a mixing bowl, toss the halved Brussels sprouts with olive oil, salt, and pepper until evenly coated.
2. **Preheat the Air Fryer:** Preheat your air fryer to 375°F (190°C).
3. **Cook the Brussels Sprouts:** Place the Brussels sprouts in the air fryer basket in a single layer. Cook at 375°F for 12-15 minutes, shaking the basket halfway through, until the sprouts are golden and crispy on the edges.
4. **Make the Balsamic Glaze:** While the Brussels sprouts are cooking, prepare the glaze. In a small saucepan, combine balsamic vinegar, honey (or maple syrup), minced garlic, salt, and black pepper. Bring to a simmer over medium heat and cook for 5-7 minutes, until the glaze is reduced and slightly thickened.
5. **Glaze the Brussels Sprouts:** Once the Brussels sprouts are done, transfer them to a mixing bowl and drizzle with the balsamic glaze. Toss to coat evenly.
6. **Serve:** Transfer the glazed Brussels sprouts to a serving dish.
7. **Serve immediately:** Enjoy as a side dish with your favorite main course.

Servings: 4
Prep time: 10 minutes
Cooking time: 15 minutes

Nutritional info:
Calories: 150
Protein: 3g
Carbs: 18g
Fat: 8g

Quick tips:

- **Crispier Sprouts:** For extra crispy sprouts, make sure they are spaced out in the air fryer basket.
- **Glaze Variations:** Add a splash of soy sauce or a pinch of red pepper flakes to the glaze for an extra depth of flavor.
- **Serving Suggestion:** Garnish with toasted almonds or shaved Parmesan for added texture and richness.

Chickpea and Spinach Fritters with Harissa

Air Fryer Chickpea and Spinach Fritters are a flavorful and nutritious snack or appetizer, packed with protein-rich chickpeas and vibrant spinach. These fritters are crispy on the outside and tender on the inside, and they pair perfectly with a spicy harissa sauce for dipping.

Tools needed:

Air fryer
Food processor
Mixing bowl
Knife and cutting board
Small bowl for harissa

Ingredients:

For the Fritters:

- 1 can (15 oz) chickpeas, drained and rinsed
- 1 cup fresh spinach, chopped
- 1/4 cup onion, finely chopped
- 2 cloves garlic, minced
- 1/4 cup breadcrumbs
- 1 tbsp fresh parsley, chopped
- 1 tbsp fresh cilantro, chopped
- 1 tsp ground cumin
- 1/2 tsp ground coriander
- 1/2 tsp smoked paprika
- 1 egg, lightly beaten
- Salt and pepper to taste
- Olive oil spray

For the Harissa Sauce:

- 2 tbsp harissa paste
- 1/4 cup Greek yogurt or sour cream
- 1 tbsp lemon juice
- Salt to taste

Directions:

1. **Prepare the Fritters:** In a food processor, pulse the chickpeas until they are broken down but not completely smooth. Transfer to a mixing bowl and add chopped spinach, onion, garlic, breadcrumbs, parsley, cilantro, cumin, coriander, smoked paprika, egg, salt, and pepper. Mix until well combined.
2. **Shape the Fritters:** Form the mixture into small patties or balls, about 1-2 inches in diameter.
3. **Preheat the Air Fryer:** Preheat your air fryer to 375°F (190°C).
4. **Cook the Fritters:** Place the fritters in the air fryer basket in a single layer. Lightly spray with olive oil. Cook at 375°F for 10-12 minutes, turning halfway through, until the fritters are golden brown and crispy.
5. **Make the Harissa Sauce:** While the fritters are cooking, prepare the harissa sauce. In a small bowl, combine harissa paste, Greek yogurt (or sour cream), lemon juice, and salt. Stir until smooth.
6. **Serve:** Transfer the crispy fritters to a serving plate and serve with harissa sauce on the side.
7. **Serve immediately:** Enjoy as an appetizer or snack.

Servings: 4 | **Prep time:** 15 minutes | **Cooking time:** 12 minutes

Nutritional info: Calories: 180, Protein: 7g, Carbs: 24g, Fat: 6g

Quick tips:

- **Consistency:** If the fritter mixture is too wet, add more breadcrumbs; if too dry, add a little water or olive oil.
- **Spice Level:** Adjust the amount of harissa paste in the sauce to suit your spice preference.
- **Serving Suggestion:** Pair with a fresh cucumber and tomato salad for a light, refreshing meal.

Stuffed Portobello Mushrooms with Goat Cheese and Pesto

Stuffed Portobello Mushrooms with Goat Cheese and Pesto is a rich and savory dish that highlights the meaty texture of Portobello mushrooms. Filled with creamy goat cheese and vibrant pesto, these mushrooms are perfect as a satisfying vegetarian main course or a flavorful side dish.

Tools needed:

Air fryer
Mixing bowl
Knife and cutting board
Spoon for stuffing

Ingredients:

- 4 large Portobello mushrooms, stems removed and gills scraped out
- 4 oz goat cheese, softened
- 2 tbsp pesto (store-bought or homemade)
- 1/4 cup breadcrumbs
- 2 tbsp grated Parmesan cheese
- 1 tbsp olive oil
- Salt and pepper to taste
- Fresh basil leaves for garnish (optional)

Directions:

1. **Prepare the Mushrooms:** Clean the Portobello mushrooms by wiping them with a damp paper towel. Remove the stems and gently scrape out the gills with a spoon to create space for the filling.
2. **Prepare the Filling:** In a mixing bowl, combine the softened goat cheese and pesto. Mix until smooth and well blended. Season with salt and pepper to taste.
3. **Stuff the Mushrooms:** Spoon the goat cheese and pesto mixture into the cavity of each mushroom, spreading it evenly. In a small bowl, mix the breadcrumbs and Parmesan cheese together, then sprinkle this mixture over the top of each stuffed mushroom.
4. **Preheat the Air Fryer:** Preheat your air fryer to 375°F (190°C).
5. **Cook the Mushrooms:** Lightly brush the outside of the mushrooms with olive oil to help them crisp up. Place the stuffed mushrooms in the air fryer basket in a single layer. Cook at 375°F for 10-12 minutes, until the mushrooms are tender and the breadcrumb topping is golden brown and crispy.
6. **Serve:** Remove the mushrooms from the air fryer and transfer to a serving plate. Garnish with fresh basil leaves if desired.
7. **Serve immediately:** Enjoy as a main dish with a side salad or as a hearty side to your favorite entrée.

Servings: 4
Prep time: 10 minutes
Cooking time: 12 minutes

Nutritional info:
Calories: 180
Protein: 7g
Carbs: 10g
Fat: 12g

Quick tips:

- **Pesto Variations:** Use different types of pesto, such as sun-dried tomato or arugula pesto, to change up the flavor profile.
- **Extra Filling:** For added texture, mix in chopped walnuts or pine nuts into the goat cheese filling.
- **Serving Suggestion:** Pair with a light white wine or a crisp salad for a balanced meal.

AIRFRYER BEEF RECIPES

Air Fryer Beef Heart Skewers with Chimichurri

Air Fryer Beef Heart Skewers with Chimichurri is a flavorful and nutrient-dense dish that makes the most of beef heart's rich taste and tender texture.

Tools needed:

Air fryer
Mixing bowl
Skewers (metal or soaked wooden skewers)
Knife and cutting board
Small bowl for chimichurri

Ingredients:

For the Beef Heart Skewers:

- 1 lb beef heart, trimmed and cut into 1-inch cubes
- 3 cloves garlic, minced
- 2 tbsp olive oil
- 1 tbsp red wine vinegar
- 1 tsp smoked paprika
- 1 tsp ground cumin
- 1/2 tsp black pepper
- 1/2 tsp salt

For the Chimichurri Sauce:

- 1/2 cup fresh parsley, finely chopped
- 1/4 cup fresh cilantro, finely chopped
- 3 cloves garlic, minced
- 1/4 cup red wine vinegar
- 1/2 cup olive oil
- 1 tsp red pepper flakes (optional)
- Salt and pepper to taste

Directions:

Prepare the Marinade: In a mixing bowl, combine minced garlic, olive oil, red wine vinegar, smoked paprika, ground cumin, black pepper, and salt. Add the beef heart cubes and toss to coat. Marinate for at least 1 hour, preferably overnight, in the refrigerator.
Preheat the Air Fryer: Preheat your air fryer to 400°F (200°C).
Assemble the Skewers: Thread the marinated beef heart cubes onto skewers, leaving a little space between each piece for even cooking.
Cook the Skewers: Place the skewers in the air fryer basket in a single layer. Cook at 400°F for 8-10 minutes, turning halfway through, until the beef heart is cooked to your desired level of doneness.
Make the Chimichurri Sauce: While the skewers are cooking, prepare the chimichurri sauce. In a small bowl, combine chopped parsley, cilantro, minced garlic, red wine vinegar, olive oil, red pepper flakes (if using), salt, and pepper. Stir until well combined.
Serve: Remove the skewers from the air fryer and let them rest for a minute. Serve with chimichurri sauce on the side.
Serve immediately: Enjoy as an appetizer or main dish.

Servings: 4 | **Prep time:** 15 minutes (plus marinating time) | **Cooking time:** 10 minutes

Nutritional info: Calories: 250, Protein: 22g, Carbs: 2g, Fat: 18g

Quick tips:

- **Marination:** The longer the beef heart marinates, the more flavorful and tender it will be.
- **Chimichurri Storage:** Chimichurri can be made ahead of time and stored in the refrigerator for up to a week.

Crispy Air Fryer Beef Tongue Tacos

Crispy Air Fryer Beef Tongue Tacos are a unique and delicious take on traditional tacos. The beef tongue is cooked until tender, then sliced and crisped in the air fryer for a rich, melt-in-your-mouth texture. Topped with fresh salsa, onions, and cilantro, these tacos are perfect for a flavorful and adventurous meal.

Tools needed:

Air fryer
Large pot for boiling tongue
Mixing bowls
Knife and cutting board
Tongs

Ingredients:

For the Beef Tongue:

- 1 beef tongue (about 2-3 lbs)
- 1 onion, quartered
- 3 cloves garlic
- 2 bay leaves
- 1 tbsp salt
- Water for boiling

For the Tacos:

- Corn tortillas
- 1 cup salsa (your choice of red or green)
- 1 small onion, finely chopped
- Fresh cilantro, chopped
- Lime wedges for serving

Directions:

1. **Cook the Beef Tongue:** Place the beef tongue, onion, garlic, bay leaves, and salt in a large pot. Cover with water and bring to a boil. Reduce the heat and simmer for 2-3 hours, or until the tongue is tender and can be easily pierced with a fork.
2. **Peel and Slice:** Once the tongue is tender, remove it from the pot and let it cool slightly. Peel off the outer skin and discard. Slice the tongue into thin strips.
3. **Preheat the Air Fryer:** Preheat your air fryer to 400°F (200°C).
4. **Crisp the Tongue Slices:** Place the tongue slices in the air fryer basket in a single layer. Cook at 400°F for 8-10 minutes, turning halfway through, until the slices are crispy on the edges.
5. **Assemble the Tacos:** Warm the corn tortillas and fill each with crispy beef tongue slices. Top with salsa, chopped onions, and cilantro.
6. **Serve:** Serve the tacos with lime wedges on the side.
7. **Serve immediately:** Enjoy as a flavorful and unique taco experience.

Servings: 4-6
Prep time: 20 minutes (plus cooking time for tongue)
Cooking time: 10 minutes

Nutritional info:
Calories: 250
Protein: 20g
Carbs: 15g
Fat: 12g

Quick tips:

- **Tenderizing Tongue:** For extra flavor, add spices like cumin, cloves, or peppercorns to the boiling water.
- **Taco Variations:** Add avocado, radishes, or pickled onions for extra flavor and texture.
- **Serving Suggestion:** Pair with a cold beer or a refreshing margarita.

Korean BBQ Beef Short Ribs

Korean BBQ Beef Short Ribs, also known as "Galbi," are a flavorful and tender dish that features marinated beef short ribs cooked to perfection in the air fryer.

Tools needed:

Air fryer
Mixing bowl
Knife and cutting board
Basting brush

Ingredients:

For the Marinade:

- 1/4 cup soy sauce
- 2 tbsp brown sugar
- 2 tbsp sesame oil
- 2 cloves garlic, minced
- 1 tbsp fresh ginger, grated
- 1 tbsp rice vinegar
- 1 tbsp honey
- 1 tsp sesame seeds
- 1/4 tsp black pepper

For the Short Ribs:

- 2 lbs beef short ribs, flanken-cut (thinly sliced across the bone)
- 2 green onions, chopped (for garnish)
- Additional sesame seeds (for garnish)

Directions:

1. **Prepare the Marinade:** In a mixing bowl, combine soy sauce, brown sugar, sesame oil, minced garlic, grated ginger, rice vinegar, honey, sesame seeds, and black pepper. Mix until the sugar is dissolved and the marinade is well combined.
2. **Marinate the Short Ribs:** Place the short ribs in a large resealable bag or shallow dish. Pour the marinade over the ribs, ensuring they are fully coated. Marinate in the refrigerator for at least 2 hours, preferably overnight.
3. **Preheat the Air Fryer:** Preheat your air fryer to 400°F (200°C).
4. **Cook the Short Ribs:** Remove the short ribs from the marinade and place them in the air fryer basket in a single layer. Cook at 400°F for 8-10 minutes, flipping halfway through, until the ribs are caramelized and cooked to your desired level of doneness.
5. **Garnish:** Remove the ribs from the air fryer and sprinkle with chopped green onions and additional sesame seeds.
6. **Serve:** Serve the short ribs with steamed rice, kimchi, and other Korean side dishes.
7. **Serve immediately:** Enjoy as a main dish with your favorite Korean accompaniments.

Servings: 4 | **Prep time:** 15 minutes (plus marinating time) | **Cooking time:** 10 minutes

Nutritional info: Calories: 450, Protein: 25g, Carbs: 12g, Fat: 35g
Quick tips:

- **Marination:** The longer the short ribs marinate, the more flavorful they will be. Overnight marination is ideal.
- **Cooking Tip:** If the ribs are too fatty, trim some of the excess fat before marinating.
- **Serving Suggestion:** Pair with traditional Korean sides like kimchi, pickled vegetables, and rice for an authentic meal.

Beef Jerky with Sichuan Peppercorn

Air Fryer Beef Jerky with Sichuan Peppercorn is a flavorful and spicy snack that combines the classic chewiness of beef jerky with the unique numbing heat of Sichuan peppercorns. This jerky is perfect for adventurous snackers who enjoy bold and complex flavors.

Tools needed:

Air fryer
Mixing bowl
Knife and cutting board
Mortar and pestle or spice grinder

Ingredients:

- 1 lb beef (such as top round or flank steak), sliced thinly against the grain
- 1/4 cup soy sauce
- 2 tbsp rice vinegar
- 1 tbsp honey
- 1 tbsp Sichuan peppercorns, toasted and ground
- 1 tsp ground ginger
- 2 cloves garlic, minced
- 1 tsp red pepper flakes (optional, for extra heat)
- 1 tsp sesame oil

Directions:

1. **Prepare the Marinade:** In a mixing bowl, combine soy sauce, rice vinegar, honey, ground Sichuan peppercorns, ground ginger, minced garlic, red pepper flakes (if using), and sesame oil. Mix well to create the marinade.
2. **Marinate the Beef:** Add the thinly sliced beef to the marinade, ensuring each piece is fully coated. Cover and refrigerate for at least 4 hours, preferably overnight, to allow the flavors to penetrate the meat.
3. **Preheat the Air Fryer**: Preheat your air fryer to 180°F (80°C), the lowest setting available.
4. **Prepare the Beef for Drying:** Lay the marinated beef slices in a single layer in the air fryer basket. Do not overlap the slices to ensure even drying.
5. **Dehydrate the Beef:** Air fry the beef at 180°F (80°C) for 3-4 hours, checking periodically to ensure the jerky is drying evenly. The jerky is ready when it is dry, chewy, and slightly flexible without breaking.
6. **Serve:** Once the jerky is done, remove it from the air fryer and let it cool completely before storing.
7. **Serve immediately or store:** Enjoy as a snack, or store in an airtight container for up to a week.

Servings: 6
Prep time: 15 minutes (plus marinating and drying time)
Cooking time: 3-4 hours

Nutritional info:
Calories: 150
Protein: 20g
Carbs: 4g
Fat: 5g

Quick tips:

- **Slice Thickness:** For quicker drying, slice the beef as thinly as possible, about 1/8 inch thick.
- **Peppercorns:** Toast the Sichuan peppercorns before grinding to release their full flavor and aroma.
- **Storage:** Store the jerky in a cool, dry place. If storing for longer periods, consider vacuum-sealing or refrigerating.

Beef Tartare with Air Fryer Crisps

Beef Tartare is a classic and elegant dish featuring finely chopped raw beef, seasoned with a variety of bold flavors. Paired with crispy air fryer crisps, this dish offers a delightful contrast of textures and is perfect for a sophisticated appetizer or light meal.

Tools needed:

Air fryer
Mixing bowl
Knife and cutting board
Small bowl for dressing

Ingredients:

For the Beef Tartare:

- 8 oz beef tenderloin or sirloin, very finely chopped
- 1 tbsp capers, finely chopped
- 1 tbsp cornichons or pickles, finely chopped
- 1 small shallot, finely chopped
- 1 tsp Dijon mustard
- 1 tsp Worcestershire sauce
- 1 tbsp fresh parsley, chopped
- 1 egg yolk (optional, for richness)
- Salt and pepper to taste

For the Air Fryer Crisps:

- 1 large potato, thinly sliced (or use baguette slices for crostini)
- 1 tbsp olive oil
- Salt and pepper to taste

Directions:

1. **Prepare the Tartare:** In a mixing bowl, combine the finely chopped beef, capers, cornichons, shallot, Dijon mustard, Worcestershire sauce, and fresh parsley. Mix well until all ingredients are evenly distributed. Season with salt and pepper to taste.
2. **Preheat the Air Fryer:** Preheat your air fryer to 375°F (190°C).
3. **Make the Crisps:** Toss the thinly sliced potatoes or baguette slices with olive oil, salt, and pepper. Arrange them in a single layer in the air fryer basket. Air fry at 375°F for 8-10 minutes, turning halfway through, until the crisps are golden brown and crispy.
4. **Assemble the Dish:** If using, gently fold the egg yolk into the tartare mixture just before serving for added richness.
5. **Serve:** Plate the beef tartare in a small mound or shaped using a ring mold. Serve alongside the air fryer crisps.
6. **Serve immediately:** Enjoy as an appetizer or light meal.

Servings: 4
Prep time: 20 minutes
Cooking time: 10 minutes

Nutritional info:
Calories: 250
Protein: 18g
Carbs: 15g
Fat: 14g

Quick tips:

- **High-Quality Beef:** Use the freshest, highest quality beef for tartare, and keep it very cold until just before serving.
- **Crisp Variety:** Experiment with different vegetables or breads for the crisps, such as sweet potatoes, beets, or baguette slices.
- **Serving Suggestion:** Garnish with extra capers, parsley, and a drizzle of olive oil for added presentation.

Air Fryer Bone Marrow with Garlic and Parsley

Air Fryer Bone Marrow with Garlic and Parsley is a rich, indulgent dish that celebrates the creamy texture and robust flavor of bone marrow. Roasted in the air fryer until bubbly and golden, the marrow is then topped with a fresh garlic and parsley mixture, creating a perfect spread for crusty bread.

Tools needed:

Air fryer
Knife and cutting board
Small bowl for parsley mixture
Spoon for scooping marrow

Ingredients:

- 4 beef marrow bones, cut lengthwise or crosswise (about 2-3 inches each)
- 2 cloves garlic, minced
- 2 tbsp fresh parsley, chopped
- 1 tbsp lemon juice
- 1 tbsp olive oil
- Salt and pepper to taste
- Crusty bread for serving

Directions:

1. **Prepare the Bones:** Season the marrow bones with salt and pepper. Place them in the air fryer basket, marrow side up.
2. **Preheat the Air Fryer:** Preheat your air fryer to 400°F (200°C).
3. **Cook the Bones:** Air fry the marrow bones at 400°F for 10-12 minutes, or until the marrow is bubbly and lightly browned.
4. **Prepare the Garlic and Parsley Topping:** While the marrow is cooking, combine minced garlic, chopped parsley, lemon juice, olive oil, salt, and pepper in a small bowl. Mix well.
5. **Top the Marrow:** Once the marrow bones are done, remove them from the air fryer. Immediately spoon the garlic and parsley mixture over the hot marrow.
6. **Serve:** Serve the bone marrow with crusty bread, using a spoon to scoop out the marrow and spread it onto the bread.
7. **Serve immediately:** Enjoy as a decadent appetizer or side dish.

Servings: 4
Prep time: 10 minutes
Cooking time: 12 minutes

Nutritional info:
Calories: 300
Protein: 8g
Carbs: 10g
Fat: 26g

Quick tips:

- **Bone Selection:** Ask your butcher for center-cut marrow bones for the best presentation and flavor.
- **Serving Suggestion:** Serve with pickled onions or a side salad to cut through the richness of the marrow.
- **Leftovers:** If you have leftover marrow, stir it into mashed potatoes or spread it on toast for a luxurious treat.

Beef Empanadas with Chimichurri

Air Fryer Beef Empanadas are a delicious and convenient take on a traditional Latin American favorite. These empanadas feature a savory ground beef filling encased in a crispy, golden pastry shell.

Tools needed:

Air fryer
Mixing bowls
Knife and cutting board
Rolling pin (if using homemade dough)
Pastry brush

Ingredients:
For the Empanadas:
1 lb ground beef
1 small onion, finely chopped
2 cloves garlic, minced
1 tsp ground cumin
1 tsp smoked paprika
1/2 tsp ground oregano
1/4 tsp red pepper flakes (optional, for heat)
1/2 cup green olives, chopped
1/4 cup raisins (optional)
1/4 cup tomato paste
Salt and pepper to taste
12-16 empanada dough discs (store-bought or homemade)
1 egg, beaten (for egg wash)
For the Chimichurri Sauce:
1/2 cup fresh parsley, finely chopped
1/4 cup fresh cilantro, finely chopped
3 cloves garlic, minced
1/4 cup red wine vinegar
1/2 cup olive oil
1 tsp red pepper flakes (optional)
Salt and pepper to taste

Directions:
Prepare the Beef Filling: In a skillet over medium heat, cook the ground beef until browned. Add the chopped onion, minced garlic, ground cumin, smoked paprika, oregano, and red pepper flakes (if using). Cook for 5-7 minutes until the onions are soft. Stir in the chopped olives, raisins (if using), and tomato paste. Season with salt and pepper. Cook for another 2-3 minutes until everything is well combined. Remove from heat and let cool slightly.
Assemble the Empanadas: Place a spoonful of the beef filling in the center of each empanada dough disc. Fold the dough over to create a half-moon shape and press the edges together to seal. Use a fork to crimp the edges. Brush the tops with beaten egg.
Preheat the Air Fryer: Preheat your air fryer to 375°F (190°C).
Cook the Empanadas: Arrange the empanadas in the air fryer basket in a single layer. Cook at 375°F for 8-10 minutes, until the empanadas are golden brown and crispy.
Make the Chimichurri Sauce: While the empanadas are cooking, prepare the chimichurri sauce. In a small bowl, combine parsley, cilantro, minced garlic, red wine vinegar, olive oil, red pepper flakes (if using), salt, and pepper. Stir until well mixed.
Serve: Remove the empanadas from the air fryer and let them cool slightly. Serve with chimichurri sauce on the side for dipping.

Servings: 4-6 | **Prep time:** 20 minutes | **Cooking time:** 10 minutes

Nutritional info: Calories: 300, Protein: 12g, Carbs: 25g, Fat: 16g

Quick tips:

- **Empanada Dough:** If using store-bought dough, make sure to thaw it according to the package instructions before assembling.
- **Filling Variations:** Feel free to add other ingredients to the filling, such as hard-boiled eggs or cheese, for extra flavor.

Spicy Air Fryer Beef and Kimchi Stuffed Peppers

Spicy Air Fryer Beef and Kimchi Stuffed Peppers are a fusion dish that brings together savory ground beef, tangy kimchi, and tender bell peppers. The filling is rich in flavor and spice, making these stuffed peppers a satisfying and unique meal with a Korean twist.

Tools needed:

Air fryer
Mixing bowl
Knife and cutting board
Spoon for stuffing

Ingredients:

- 4 large bell peppers, tops cut off and seeds removed
- 1 lb ground beef
- 1 cup kimchi, chopped
- 1 small onion, finely chopped
- 2 cloves garlic, minced
- 1 tbsp gochujang (Korean chili paste) or sriracha
- 1 tbsp soy sauce
- 1 tsp sesame oil
- 1/2 cup cooked rice (optional, for added texture)
- 2 green onions, chopped (for garnish)
- Sesame seeds (for garnish)

Directions:

1. **Prepare the Filling:** In a skillet over medium heat, cook the ground beef until browned. Add the chopped onion and minced garlic, and cook for 5-7 minutes until the onions are soft. Stir in the chopped kimchi, gochujang (or sriracha), soy sauce, and sesame oil. If using rice, stir it in at this stage. Cook for another 2-3 minutes until everything is well combined. Remove from heat.
2. **Stuff the Peppers:** Spoon the beef and kimchi mixture into the hollowed-out bell peppers, packing the filling down slightly.
3. **Preheat the Air Fryer:** Preheat your air fryer to 375°F (190°C).
4. **Cook the Stuffed Peppers:** Place the stuffed peppers in the air fryer basket in a single layer. Cook at 375°F for 15-18 minutes, until the peppers are tender and slightly charred on the edges.
5. **Garnish:** Remove the stuffed peppers from the air fryer and garnish with chopped green onions and sesame seeds.
6. **Serve:** Serve the stuffed peppers hot as a main course.
7. **Serve immediately:** Enjoy the flavorful and spicy combination of beef and kimchi in these stuffed peppers.

Servings: 4
Prep time: 15 minutes
Cooking time: 18 minutes

Nutritional info:
Calories: 350
Protein: 20g
Carbs: 18g
Fat: 22g

Quick tips:

- **Spice Level:** Adjust the amount of gochujang or sriracha based on your preferred spice level.
- **Kimchi:** For extra flavor, use well-fermented kimchi in this recipe.
- **Serving Suggestion:** Pair with a side of steamed rice or a light cucumber salad for a balanced meal.

AIRFRYER APPETIZERS & SNACKS RECIPES

Air Fryer Crispy Chickpeas with Za'atar

Air Fryer Crispy Chickpeas with Za'atar is a healthy and flavorful snack that combines the crunch of roasted chickpeas with the aromatic and tangy flavors of za'atar, a Middle Eastern spice blend. These chickpeas are perfect for snacking, topping salads, or adding a crunchy element to your favorite dishes.

Tools needed:

Air fryer
Mixing bowl
Baking sheet (optional, for drying chickpeas)
Spoon for tossing

Ingredients:

- 1 can (15 oz) chickpeas, drained, rinsed, and thoroughly dried
- 1 tbsp olive oil
- 1-2 tbsp za'atar spice blend
- Salt to taste

Directions:

1. **Dry the Chickpeas:** After rinsing, spread the chickpeas out on a baking sheet and pat them dry with a paper towel. Let them air dry for about 10 minutes to ensure they are completely dry, which helps them crisp up in the air fryer.
2. **Season the Chickpeas:** In a mixing bowl, toss the dried chickpeas with olive oil, za'atar, and salt until they are evenly coated.
3. **Preheat the Air Fryer:** Preheat your air fryer to 375°F (190°C).
4. **Cook the Chickpeas:** Place the seasoned chickpeas in the air fryer basket in a single layer. Cook at 375°F for 12-15 minutes, shaking the basket halfway through, until the chickpeas are golden brown and crispy.
5. **Cool and Serve:** Remove the chickpeas from the air fryer and let them cool slightly. They will continue to crisp up as they cool.
6. **Serve immediately:** Enjoy as a snack or use as a topping for salads, soups, or grain bowls.

Servings: 4
Prep time: 10 minutes
Cooking time: 15 minutes

Nutritional info:
Calories: 120
Protein: 6g
Carbs: 18g
Fat: 4g

Quick tips:

- **Extra Crispiness:** For even crispier chickpeas, remove the skins before seasoning.
- **Za'atar:** If you don't have za'atar, substitute with a mix of thyme, sesame seeds, and sumac.
- **Storage:** Store leftover chickpeas in an airtight container for up to 2 days to retain their crispiness.

Air Fryer Gochujang Cauliflower Bites

Air Fryer Gochujang Cauliflower Bites are a spicy, tangy, and crispy dish that showcases the bold flavors of Korean cuisine. The cauliflower florets are coated in a gochujang-based sauce and air-fried to perfection, making them a perfect appetizer or side dish.

Tools needed:

Air fryer
Mixing bowl
Small saucepan for sauce
Tongs for tossing

Ingredients:

- 1 medium head of cauliflower, cut into florets
- 1/4 cup gochujang (Korean chili paste)
- 2 tbsp soy sauce
- 2 tbsp honey or maple syrup
- 1 tbsp rice vinegar
- 1 tbsp sesame oil
- 2 cloves garlic, minced
- 1 tsp ginger, grated
- 1 tbsp sesame seeds (for garnish)
- Chopped green onions (for garnish)

Directions:

1. **Prepare the Sauce:** In a small saucepan over medium heat, combine gochujang, soy sauce, honey (or maple syrup), rice vinegar, sesame oil, minced garlic, and grated ginger. Stir well and cook for 2-3 minutes until the sauce is heated through and slightly thickened.
2. **Toss the Cauliflower:** In a mixing bowl, toss the cauliflower florets with the prepared gochujang sauce until evenly coated.
3. **Preheat the Air Fryer:** Preheat your air fryer to 375°F (190°C).
4. **Cook the Cauliflower:** Place the coated cauliflower florets in the air fryer basket in a single layer. Cook at 375°F for 12-15 minutes, shaking the basket halfway through, until the cauliflower is crispy and slightly charred.
5. **Garnish:** Remove the cauliflower bites from the air fryer and transfer to a serving plate. Garnish with sesame seeds and chopped green onions.
6. **Serve immediately:** Enjoy as a spicy appetizer or side dish.

Servings: 4
Prep time: 10 minutes
Cooking time: 15 minutes

Nutritional info:
Calories: 140
Protein: 4g
Carbs: 18g
Fat: 6g

Quick tips:

- **Gochujang Substitute:** If you don't have gochujang, you can substitute with sriracha or another chili paste, though the flavor will be slightly different.
- **Extra Sauce:** For a saucier dish, reserve some of the sauce to drizzle over the cooked cauliflower before serving.
- **Serving Suggestion:** Pair with steamed rice or as a topping for grain bowls for a complete meal.

Air Fryer Avocado Fries with Wasabi Mayo

Air Fryer Avocado Fries are a deliciously creamy and crispy snack, perfect for dipping into a tangy and spicy wasabi mayo. The air fryer gives the avocado slices a golden crust while keeping the inside smooth and rich, making these fries an irresistible treat.

Tools needed:

Air fryer
Mixing bowls
Knife and cutting board
Small bowl for dipping sauce

Ingredients:

For the Avocado Fries:

- 2 ripe avocados, sliced into wedges
- 1/2 cup flour
- 1 egg, beaten
- 1 cup panko breadcrumbs
- 1/4 cup grated Parmesan cheese
- 1/2 tsp garlic powder
- Salt and pepper to taste
- Olive oil spray

For the Wasabi Mayo:

- 1/4 cup mayonnaise
- 1 tsp wasabi paste (adjust to taste)
- 1 tsp lemon juice
- 1 tsp soy sauce
- Salt to taste

Directions:

1. **Prepare the Breading:** In one bowl, place the flour. In another bowl, beat the egg. In a third bowl, combine panko breadcrumbs, grated Parmesan, garlic powder, salt, and pepper.
2. **Bread the Avocado:** Dredge each avocado wedge in flour, shaking off the excess. Dip it into the beaten egg, then coat with the panko mixture, pressing gently to adhere the breadcrumbs.
3. **Preheat the Air Fryer:** Preheat your air fryer to 375°F (190°C).
4. **Cook the Avocado Fries:** Arrange the breaded avocado slices in a single layer in the air fryer basket. Lightly spray with olive oil. Cook at 375°F for 8-10 minutes, flipping halfway through, until the fries are golden brown and crispy.
5. **Make the Wasabi Mayo:** While the avocado fries are cooking, prepare the dipping sauce. In a small bowl, combine mayonnaise, wasabi paste, lemon juice, soy sauce, and a pinch of salt. Stir until smooth.
6. **Serve:** Remove the avocado fries from the air fryer and transfer to a serving plate. Serve with wasabi mayo on the side for dipping.
7. **Serve immediately:** Enjoy as a snack or appetizer.

Servings: 4 | **Prep time:** 15 minutes | **Cooking time:** 10 minutes

Nutritional info: Calories: 220, Protein: 4g, Carbs: 18g, Fat: 16g

Quick tips:

- **Ripeness:** Use avocados that are ripe but firm to ensure they hold their shape during cooking.
- **Breading Tip:** For an extra-crispy coating, double-dip the avocado slices in egg and panko.
- **Serving Suggestion:** These avocado fries also pair well with a squeeze of lime juice or a sprinkle of chili powder for added zest.

Crispy Halloumi Fries with Honey

Crispy Halloumi Fries with Honey is a delicious and indulgent appetizer that combines the savory, salty flavor of halloumi cheese with a crispy exterior and a drizzle of sweet honey. These fries are perfect for snacking or as a unique starter to a meal.

Tools needed:

Air fryer
Mixing bowl
Knife and cutting board
Tongs

Ingredients:

- 1 block of halloumi cheese (about 8 oz)
- 1/4 cup flour
- 1/2 tsp smoked paprika
- 1/4 tsp garlic powder
- Olive oil spray
- 2 tbsp honey (for drizzling)
- Fresh herbs for garnish (optional)

Directions:

1. **Prepare the Halloumi:** Cut the block of halloumi into fry-shaped sticks, about 1/2 inch thick.
2. **Prepare the Breading:** In a mixing bowl, combine the flour, smoked paprika, and garlic powder. Dredge each halloumi stick in the flour mixture, ensuring an even coating.
3. **Preheat the Air Fryer:** Preheat your air fryer to 375°F (190°C).
4. **Cook the Halloumi Fries:** Arrange the coated halloumi sticks in the air fryer basket in a single layer. Lightly spray with olive oil. Cook at 375°F for 8-10 minutes, turning halfway through, until the halloumi is golden and crispy.
5. **Serve:** Remove the halloumi fries from the air fryer and transfer to a serving plate. Drizzle with honey and garnish with fresh herbs if desired.
6. **Serve immediately:** Enjoy as a snack or appetizer, perfect for dipping or eating on their own.

Servings: 4
Prep time: 10 minutes
Cooking time: 10 minutes

Nutritional info:
Calories: 250
Protein: 12g
Carbs: 15g
Fat: 18g

Quick tips:

- **Flour Coating:** For an extra crispy texture, double-dip the halloumi in flour.
- **Serving Suggestion:** Pair with a side of yogurt or a spicy dipping sauce for contrast.
- **Variation:** Sprinkle some chili flakes over the halloumi before serving for a spicy kick.

Air Fryer Beet Chips with Goat Cheese Dip

Air Fryer Beet Chips are a healthy and vibrant snack that offers a satisfying crunch with a naturally sweet flavor. Paired with a creamy goat cheese dip, these chips are perfect for a sophisticated appetizer or a guilt-free snack.

Tools needed:

Air fryer
Mandoline or sharp knife
Mixing bowls
Small bowl for dip

Ingredients:

For the Beet Chips:

- 3 medium beets, peeled and thinly sliced
- 1 tbsp olive oil
- Salt to taste
- Fresh thyme for garnish (optional)

For the Goat Cheese Dip:

- 4 oz goat cheese, softened
- 2 tbsp Greek yogurt or sour cream
- 1 tbsp honey
- 1 tsp lemon juice
- Salt and pepper to taste

Directions:

1. **Prepare the Beets:** Using a mandoline or sharp knife, slice the beets into thin, even slices. Toss the beet slices in a mixing bowl with olive oil and salt until evenly coated.
2. **Preheat the Air Fryer:** Preheat your air fryer to 320°F (160°C).
3. **Cook the Beet Chips:** Arrange the beet slices in the air fryer basket in a single layer. Cook at 320°F for 15-18 minutes, shaking the basket occasionally, until the chips are crispy. You may need to cook in batches to avoid overcrowding.
4. **Make the Goat Cheese Dip:** While the beet chips are cooking, prepare the dip. In a small bowl, combine softened goat cheese, Greek yogurt (or sour cream), honey, lemon juice, salt, and pepper. Stir until smooth and creamy.
5. **Serve:** Transfer the beet chips to a serving plate and garnish with fresh thyme if desired. Serve with the goat cheese dip on the side.
6. **Serve immediately:** Enjoy as a healthy snack or appetizer.

Servings: 4
Prep time: 15 minutes
Cooking time: 18 minutes

Nutritional info:
Calories: 120
Protein: 5g
Carbs: 12g
Fat: 7g

Quick tips:

- **Slice Evenly:** Use a mandoline to ensure the beet slices are even, which helps them cook uniformly.
- **Crispier Chips:** Let the chips cool completely before serving; they will crisp up more as they cool.
- **Variation:** Add fresh herbs like rosemary or thyme to the beet chips before cooking for extra flavor.

Stuffed Jalapeños with Goat Cheese and Bacon

Air Fryer Stuffed Jalapeños with Goat Cheese and Bacon is a spicy, creamy, and savory appetizer that combines the heat of jalapeños with the richness of goat cheese and the smoky flavor of crispy bacon. These stuffed peppers are perfect for parties, game day, or any time you want a flavorful bite.

Tools needed:

Air fryer
Mixing bowl
Knife and cutting board
Spoon for stuffing

Ingredients:

- 8 large jalapeños, halved and seeds removed
- 4 oz goat cheese, softened
- 4 slices bacon, cooked and crumbled
- 1/4 cup shredded cheddar cheese
- 1 tbsp fresh chives, chopped
- Salt and pepper to taste
- Olive oil spray

Directions:

1. **Prepare the Filling:** In a mixing bowl, combine softened goat cheese, crumbled bacon, shredded cheddar cheese, chopped chives, salt, and pepper. Mix until well combined.
2. **Stuff the Jalapeños:** Spoon the goat cheese mixture into each halved jalapeño, filling them generously.
3. **Preheat the Air Fryer:** Preheat your air fryer to 375°F (190°C).
4. **Cook the Stuffed Jalapeños:** Arrange the stuffed jalapeños in the air fryer basket in a single layer. Lightly spray with olive oil. Cook at 375°F for 8-10 minutes, until the jalapeños are tender and the cheese is bubbly and golden.
5. **Serve:** Remove the stuffed jalapeños from the air fryer and transfer to a serving plate.
6. **Serve immediately:** Enjoy as a spicy and creamy appetizer or snack.

Servings: 4
Prep time: 15 minutes
Cooking time: 10 minutes

Nutritional info:
Calories: 180
Protein: 7g
Carbs: 4g
Fat: 15g

Quick tips:

- **Heat Level:** For less heat, remove the seeds and membranes from the jalapeños before stuffing.
- **Cheese Variations:** Substitute the goat cheese with cream cheese for a milder flavor.
- **Serving Suggestion:** Garnish with extra chopped chives or a drizzle of sour cream for added flavor.

Crispy Air Fryer Nori Seaweed Chips

Crispy Air Fryer Nori Seaweed Chips are a light and savory snack that offers a satisfying crunch with the umami-rich flavor of seaweed. These chips are easy to make and perfect for a quick, healthy treat.

Tools needed:

Air fryer
Scissors or knife
Small brush or spoon for oil

Ingredients:

- 6 sheets of nori seaweed
- 2 tbsp sesame oil (or olive oil)
- 1 tsp soy sauce (optional, for extra flavor)
- 1 tsp sesame seeds (optional, for garnish)
- Salt to taste

Directions:

1. **Prepare the Nori:** Cut the nori sheets into smaller rectangles or squares using scissors or a knife, depending on your preferred chip size.
2. **Season the Nori:** In a small bowl, mix the sesame oil and soy sauce (if using). Lightly brush or spoon a thin layer of the oil mixture onto one side of each nori piece. Sprinkle with a little salt and sesame seeds, if desired.
3. **Preheat the Air Fryer:** Preheat your air fryer to 300°F (150°C).
4. **Cook the Nori Chips:** Place the nori pieces in the air fryer basket in a single layer, being careful not to overlap them. Air fry at 300°F for 3-5 minutes, or until the nori is crispy and lightly browned around the edges. Keep an eye on them as they can burn quickly.
5. **Cool and Serve:** Remove the nori chips from the air fryer and let them cool on a wire rack.
6. **Serve immediately:** Enjoy as a snack on their own or as a crunchy topping for salads or rice bowls.

Servings: 2-4
Prep time: 5 minutes
Cooking time: 5 minutes

Nutritional info:
Calories: 80
Protein: 2g
Carbs: 4g
Fat: 7g

Quick tips:

- **Watch Closely:** Nori can burn easily, so monitor closely during cooking.
- **Season Variations:** Experiment with different seasonings like chili flakes, garlic powder, or nutritional yeast for extra flavor.
- **Serving Suggestion:** Pair with a dipping sauce like soy sauce or wasabi mayo for added depth of flavor.

Spicy Air Fryer Plantain Chips

Spicy Air Fryer Plantain Chips are a delicious and crunchy snack with a hint of sweetness and a spicy kick. These chips are healthier than store-bought versions and are perfect for dipping or enjoying on their own.

Tools needed:

Air fryer
Knife and cutting board
Mandoline (optional, for even slices)
Mixing bowl

Ingredients:

- 2 green plantains, peeled and thinly sliced
- 2 tbsp olive oil or coconut oil
- 1 tsp chili powder
- 1/2 tsp paprika
- 1/2 tsp garlic powder
- 1/4 tsp cayenne pepper (optional, for extra heat)
- Salt to taste

Directions:

1. **Prepare the Plantains:** Peel the plantains and slice them into thin rounds or diagonally for longer chips. Using a mandoline can help achieve even thickness.
2. **Season the Plantains:** In a mixing bowl, toss the plantain slices with olive oil, chili powder, paprika, garlic powder, cayenne pepper (if using), and salt. Ensure the slices are evenly coated with the seasoning.
3. **Preheat the Air Fryer:** Preheat your air fryer to 350°F (175°C).
4. **Cook the Plantain Chips:** Arrange the plantain slices in a single layer in the air fryer basket. Cook at 350°F for 8-10 minutes, flipping halfway through, until the chips are golden brown and crispy. You may need to cook them in batches depending on the size of your air fryer.
5. **Cool and Serve:** Once the plantain chips are done, remove them from the air fryer and let them cool on a wire rack.
6. **Serve immediately:** Enjoy as a snack or pair with your favorite dip.

Servings: 4
Prep time: 10 minutes
Cooking time: 10 minutes

Nutritional info:
Calories: 150
Protein: 1g
Carbs: 20g
Fat: 7g

Quick tips:

- **Plantain Ripeness:** Use green plantains for crispy chips; riper plantains will result in sweeter, softer chips.
- **Batch Cooking:** Avoid overcrowding the air fryer basket to ensure even cooking and crispiness.
- **Serving Suggestion:** Serve with guacamole, salsa, or a spicy aioli for a delicious snack.

AIRFRYER LOW-CARB RECIPES

Air Fryer Keto Scotch Eggs

Air Fryer Keto Scotch Eggs are a low-carb, high-protein twist on the traditional British snack. These eggs are encased in a seasoned sausage mixture and air-fried to crispy perfection, making them ideal for breakfast, a snack, or a light meal.

Tools needed:

Air fryer
Mixing bowls
Knife and cutting board
Small saucepan for boiling eggs

Ingredients:

- 4 large eggs
- 1 lb ground pork sausage (or your preferred sausage meat)
- 1/2 tsp garlic powder
- 1/2 tsp onion powder
- 1/2 tsp smoked paprika
- 1/4 tsp ground black pepper
- 1/4 tsp salt
- 1/2 cup almond flour
- 1 egg, beaten (for coating)
- Olive oil spray

Directions:

1. **Boil the Eggs:** Place the eggs in a small saucepan and cover with water. Bring to a boil, then reduce the heat and simmer for 6 minutes for soft-boiled eggs or 10 minutes for hard-boiled eggs. Immediately transfer the eggs to an ice bath to cool, then peel.
2. **Prepare the Sausage Mixture:** In a mixing bowl, combine the ground pork sausage with garlic powder, onion powder, smoked paprika, black pepper, and salt. Divide the sausage mixture into four equal portions.
3. **Wrap the Eggs:** Flatten each portion of sausage into a thin patty. Place a peeled egg in the center of each patty, then wrap the sausage around the egg, ensuring it is fully enclosed.
4. **Coat the Eggs:** Dip each sausage-covered egg in the beaten egg, then roll it in almond flour to coat.
5. **Preheat the Air Fryer:** Preheat your air fryer to 375°F (190°C).
6. **Cook the Scotch Eggs:** Lightly spray the coated eggs with olive oil and place them in the air fryer basket. Cook at 375°F for 12-15 minutes, turning halfway through, until the sausage is cooked through and the coating is crispy and golden.
7. **Serve:** Remove the Scotch eggs from the air fryer and let them cool slightly before slicing in half.
8. **Serve immediately:** Enjoy as a protein-packed breakfast or snack.

Servings: 4
Prep time: 15 minutes
Cooking time: 15 minutes

Nutritional info: Calories: 320, Protein: 22g, Carbs: 4g, Fat: 24g

Quick tips:

- **Egg Cooking:** Adjust boiling time based on your preference for soft or hard yolks.
- **Almond Flour Substitute:** Use crushed pork rinds instead of almond flour for an even lower-carb option.
- **Serving Suggestion:** Serve with a side of mustard or hot sauce for added flavor.

Air Fryer Almond-Crusted Halibut

Air Fryer Almond-Crusted Halibut is a delicious and healthy dish that features tender halibut fillets coated in a crunchy almond crust. The air fryer helps achieve a golden, crispy exterior while keeping the fish moist and flaky inside, making it a perfect choice for a light yet satisfying meal.

Tools needed:

Air fryer
Mixing bowls
Knife and cutting board
Food processor (optional, for grinding almonds)

Ingredients:

- 4 halibut fillets (about 6 oz each)
- 1/2 cup almonds, finely ground
- 1/4 cup Parmesan cheese, grated
- 1 tsp garlic powder
- 1 tsp lemon zest
- 1/2 tsp dried thyme
- 1/2 tsp salt
- 1/4 tsp ground black pepper
- 1 egg, beaten
- Olive oil spray
- Lemon wedges for serving

Directions:

1. **Prepare the Coating:** In a mixing bowl, combine ground almonds, grated Parmesan cheese, garlic powder, lemon zest, dried thyme, salt, and pepper. In a separate bowl, beat the egg.
2. **Coat the Halibut:** Dip each halibut fillet into the beaten egg, then press it into the almond mixture, ensuring an even coating on all sides.
3. **Preheat the Air Fryer:** Preheat your air fryer to 375°F (190°C).
4. **Cook the Halibut:** Lightly spray the coated fillets with olive oil and place them in the air fryer basket in a single layer. Cook at 375°F for 10-12 minutes, or until the crust is golden brown and the fish is cooked through (internal temperature of 145°F).
5. **Serve:** Remove the halibut from the air fryer and serve immediately with lemon wedges on the side.
6. **Serve immediately:** Enjoy as a main dish with a side of vegetables or a fresh salad.

Servings: 4
Prep time: 15 minutes
Cooking time: 12 minutes

Nutritional info:
Calories: 350
Protein: 34g
Carbs: 6g
Fat: 20g

Quick tips:

- **Almond Grinding:** If you don't have ground almonds, pulse whole almonds in a food processor until finely ground.
- **Fish Variety:** This recipe also works well with other white fish, like cod or tilapia.
- **Serving Suggestion:** Pair with steamed asparagus or roasted Brussels sprouts for a complete meal.

Crispy Air Fryer Cabbage Steaks with Parmesan

Crispy Air Fryer Cabbage Steaks with Parmesan are a simple yet flavorful side dish that transforms humble cabbage into a crispy, savory delight. The cabbage steaks are seasoned, air-fried to perfection, and topped with Parmesan cheese, making them a perfect accompaniment to any meal.

Tools needed:

Air fryer
Knife and cutting board
Mixing bowl
Basting brush

Ingredients:

- 1 medium head of cabbage
- 2 tbsp olive oil
- 1 tsp garlic powder
- 1 tsp smoked paprika
- Salt and pepper to taste
- 1/4 cup grated Parmesan cheese
- Fresh parsley for garnish (optional)

Directions:

1. **Prepare the Cabbage:** Slice the cabbage into thick steaks, about 1-inch thick. You should get about 4-6 steaks from a medium cabbage, depending on its size.
2. **Season the Cabbage:** In a mixing bowl, combine olive oil, garlic powder, smoked paprika, salt, and pepper. Brush both sides of each cabbage steak with the seasoned olive oil mixture.
3. **Preheat the Air Fryer:** Preheat your air fryer to 375°F (190°C).
4. **Cook the Cabbage Steaks:** Place the cabbage steaks in the air fryer basket in a single layer. Cook at 375°F for 10-12 minutes, flipping halfway through, until the edges are crispy and golden brown.
5. **Add Parmesan:** In the last 2-3 minutes of cooking, sprinkle the grated Parmesan cheese over the cabbage steaks and continue cooking until the cheese is melted and slightly browned.
6. **Serve:** Remove the cabbage steaks from the air fryer and garnish with fresh parsley if desired.
7. **Serve immediately:** Enjoy as a side dish with your favorite protein or as a vegetarian main.

Servings: 4
Prep time: 10 minutes
Cooking time: 12 minutes

Nutritional info:
Calories: 120
Protein: 4g
Carbs: 8g
Fat: 9g

Quick tips:

- **Even Cooking:** Ensure the cabbage steaks are evenly thick for uniform cooking.
- **Cheese Variation:** For a different flavor, try using shredded mozzarella or Gruyère instead of Parmesan.
- **Serving Suggestion:** Pair with roasted chicken or grilled fish for a complete meal.

Air Fryer Keto Zucchini Chips

Air Fryer Keto Zucchini Chips are a healthy, low-carb snack option that is both crispy and satisfying. These chips are seasoned and air-fried to perfection, making them a great alternative to traditional potato chips, perfect for dipping or enjoying on their own.

Tools needed:

Air fryer
Mandoline or knife for slicing
Mixing bowls
Parchment paper (optional)

Ingredients:

- 2 medium zucchinis, thinly sliced
- 2 tbsp olive oil
- 1/4 cup grated Parmesan cheese
- 1/2 tsp garlic powder
- 1/2 tsp onion powder
- 1/4 tsp smoked paprika
- Salt and pepper to taste

Directions:

1. **Prepare the Zucchini:** Slice the zucchinis thinly using a mandoline or a sharp knife. Aim for slices that are about 1/8 inch thick for the best results.
2. **Season the Zucchini:** In a mixing bowl, toss the zucchini slices with olive oil, ensuring they are evenly coated. In a separate bowl, combine Parmesan cheese, garlic powder, onion powder, smoked paprika, salt, and pepper. Sprinkle the seasoning mixture over the zucchini slices and toss to coat.
3. **Preheat the Air Fryer:** Preheat your air fryer to 350°F (175°C).
4. **Cook the Zucchini Chips:** Place the zucchini slices in the air fryer basket in a single layer. You may need to work in batches depending on the size of your air fryer. Air fry at 350°F for 10-15 minutes, shaking the basket or flipping the slices halfway through, until the chips are golden brown and crispy.
5. **Cool and Serve:** Once the zucchini chips are done, remove them from the air fryer and let them cool slightly. They will continue to crisp up as they cool.
6. **Serve immediately:** Enjoy as a keto-friendly snack or a crunchy side dish.

Servings: 4
Prep time: 10 minutes
Cooking time: 15 minutes

Nutritional info:
Calories: 100
Protein: 3g
Carbs: 5g
Fat: 8g

Quick tips:

- **Slice Thickness:** Make sure the zucchini slices are evenly thick to ensure consistent cooking and crispiness.
- **Storage:** Store leftover chips in an airtight container for up to 2 days, though they are best enjoyed fresh.
- **Serving Suggestion:** Serve with a side of keto-friendly dip, such as ranch or garlic aioli, for extra flavor.

Air Fryer Keto Cauliflower Mac and Cheese

Air Fryer Keto Cauliflower Mac and Cheese is a comforting and delicious low-carb alternative to traditional mac and cheese. This dish features tender cauliflower florets coated in a rich and creamy cheese sauce, then air-fried to create a crispy, golden topping.

Tools needed:

Air fryer
Mixing bowls
Saucepan
Baking dish (oven-safe and air fryer-friendly)
Whisk

Ingredients:

- 1 large head of cauliflower, cut into florets
- 1 cup heavy cream
- 1 1/2 cups shredded sharp cheddar cheese
- 1/2 cup grated Parmesan cheese
- 1/4 cup cream cheese
- 1 tsp Dijon mustard
- 1/2 tsp garlic powder
- 1/2 tsp onion powder
- Salt and pepper to taste
- 1/4 cup pork rinds, crushed (optional, for topping)
- 2 tbsp butter, melted (optional, for topping)

Directions:

1. **Prepare the Cauliflower:** Steam or blanch the cauliflower florets until they are tender but still firm, about 5-7 minutes. Drain and set aside.
2. **Make the Cheese Sauce:** In a saucepan over medium heat, combine heavy cream, cream cheese, and Dijon mustard. Whisk until the cream cheese is melted and the mixture is smooth. Gradually add the shredded cheddar and Parmesan cheese, whisking continuously until the cheese is fully melted and the sauce is creamy. Stir in garlic powder, onion powder, salt, and pepper.
3. **Combine Cauliflower and Sauce:** Add the cooked cauliflower florets to the cheese sauce, stirring to coat the cauliflower evenly.
4. **Transfer to Baking Dish:** Transfer the cauliflower and cheese mixture to an oven-safe, air fryer-friendly baking dish.
5. **Prepare the Topping (Optional):** In a small bowl, combine the crushed pork rinds and melted butter. Sprinkle the mixture over the top of the cauliflower mac and cheese for an extra crispy topping.
6. **Preheat the Air Fryer:** Preheat your air fryer to 375°F (190°C).
7. **Cook the Cauliflower Mac and Cheese:** Place the baking dish in the air fryer basket. Air fry at 375°F for 10-12 minutes, or until the top is golden and crispy.
8. **Serve:** Remove the dish from the air fryer and let it cool slightly before serving.

Servings: 4-6 | **Prep time:** 15 minutes | **Cooking time:** 12 minutes

Nutritional info: Calories: 350, Protein: 12g, Carbs: 8g, Fat: 30g
Quick tips:

- **Cheese Variety:** Experiment with different types of cheese, such as Gruyère or Gouda, for a unique flavor twist.
- **Extra Crunch:** If you prefer a crunchier topping, add more crushed pork rinds or substitute with almond flour mixed with Parmesan.

AIRFRYER DESSERT RECIPES

Air Fryer Banana Bread Muffins

Air Fryer Banana Bread Muffins are a quick and easy way to enjoy the classic flavor of banana bread in a portable, muffin form. These muffins are moist, fluffy, and perfect for breakfast, a snack, or dessert.

Tools needed:

Air fryer
Mixing bowls
Muffin tin or silicone muffin cups
Whisk

Ingredients:

- 2 ripe bananas, mashed
- 1/4 cup melted butter
- 1/4 cup brown sugar
- 1/4 cup granulated sugar
- 1 large egg
- 1 tsp vanilla extract
- 1 cup all-purpose flour
- 1 tsp baking soda
- 1/2 tsp baking powder
- 1/4 tsp salt
- 1/2 tsp ground cinnamon (optional)
- 1/4 cup chopped walnuts or chocolate chips (optional)

Directions:

1. **Prepare the Batter:** In a mixing bowl, combine the mashed bananas, melted butter, brown sugar, and granulated sugar. Whisk until well combined. Add the egg and vanilla extract, whisking again until smooth.
2. **Mix the Dry Ingredients:** In a separate bowl, whisk together the flour, baking soda, baking powder, salt, and cinnamon (if using).
3. **Combine Wet and Dry Ingredients:** Gradually add the dry ingredients to the wet ingredients, stirring until just combined. Be careful not to overmix. Fold in the chopped walnuts or chocolate chips if using.
4. **Preheat the Air Fryer:** Preheat your air fryer to 325°F (160°C).
5. **Prepare the Muffin Cups:** Lightly grease your muffin tin or silicone muffin cups. Fill each cup about 2/3 full with the banana bread batter.
6. **Cook the Muffins:** Place the muffin cups in the air fryer basket. Depending on the size of your air fryer, you may need to cook in batches. Air fry at 325°F for 10-12 minutes, or until a toothpick inserted into the center of a muffin comes out clean.
7. **Cool and Serve:** Remove the muffins from the air fryer and let them cool in the pan for a few minutes before transferring to a wire rack to cool completely.
8. **Serve immediately:** Enjoy as a breakfast treat, snack, or dessert.

Servings: 6-8 muffins | **Prep time:** 10 minutes | **Cooking time:** 12 minutes

Nutritional info: Calories: 150, Protein: 2g, Carbs: 25g, Fat: 6g

Quick tips:

- **Riper Bananas:** Use overripe bananas for a sweeter, more flavorful muffin.
- **Mix-ins:** Customize your muffins with different mix-ins like chopped nuts, dried fruit, or coconut flakes.
- **Storage:** Store leftovers in an airtight container for up to 3 days, or freeze for longer storage.

Air Fryer Chocolate Lava Cakes

Air Fryer Chocolate Lava Cakes are a decadent and rich dessert that features a warm, gooey chocolate center. These individual cakes are easy to make in the air fryer and are perfect for a special treat or to impress guests.

Tools needed:

Air fryer
Mixing bowls
Ramekins or silicone molds
Whisk

Ingredients:

- 1/2 cup semi-sweet chocolate chips
- 1/4 cup unsalted butter
- 1/4 cup all-purpose flour
- 1/2 cup powdered sugar
- 1/4 tsp salt
- 2 large eggs
- 1 tsp vanilla extract
- Cocoa powder or powdered sugar (for dusting)
- Whipped cream or ice cream (for serving, optional)

Directions:

1. **Melt the Chocolate:** In a microwave-safe bowl, combine the chocolate chips and butter. Microwave in 20-second intervals, stirring between each, until the chocolate and butter are completely melted and smooth.
2. **Prepare the Batter:** In a mixing bowl, whisk together the flour, powdered sugar, and salt. Add the melted chocolate mixture, eggs, and vanilla extract. Stir until just combined.
3. **Prepare the Ramekins:** Lightly grease the ramekins or silicone molds. Dust with cocoa powder or powdered sugar to prevent sticking. Divide the batter evenly among the ramekins.
4. **Preheat the Air Fryer:** Preheat your air fryer to 375°F (190°C).
5. **Cook the Lava Cakes:** Place the ramekins in the air fryer basket. Depending on the size of your air fryer, you may need to cook in batches. Air fry at 375°F for 8-10 minutes, or until the edges are set but the center is still slightly soft.
6. **Serve:** Let the lava cakes cool for 1-2 minutes before carefully running a knife around the edges to loosen. Invert the ramekins onto serving plates and gently lift to release the cakes.
7. **Serve immediately:** Dust with powdered sugar or cocoa powder and serve with whipped cream or ice cream if desired.

Servings: 4
Prep time: 10 minutes
Cooking time: 10 minutes

Nutritional info: Calories: 350, Protein: 5g, Carbs: 40g, Fat: 20g

Quick tips:

- **Timing:** Be careful not to overcook; the center should remain gooey for the perfect lava texture.
- **Customization:** Add a piece of chocolate or caramel in the center of the batter before cooking for an extra molten surprise.
- **Serving Suggestion:** Serve immediately for the best lava effect, as the center will firm up as the cakes cool.

Cinnamon Sugar Air Fryer Donuts

Cinnamon Sugar Air Fryer Donuts are a quick and easy way to enjoy the classic flavor of cinnamon sugar donuts without deep frying. These donuts are light, fluffy, and coated in a delicious cinnamon sugar mixture, making them perfect for breakfast or a sweet treat.

Tools needed:

Air fryer
Mixing bowls
Biscuit cutter or round cookie cutter
Pastry brush

Ingredients:

- 1 can of refrigerated biscuit dough (8 biscuits)
- 1/4 cup melted butter
- 1/2 cup granulated sugar
- 1 tbsp ground cinnamon

Directions:

1. **Prepare the Donuts:** Open the can of biscuit dough and separate the biscuits. Use a small biscuit cutter or a round cookie cutter to cut a hole in the center of each biscuit to create a donut shape. Save the holes to make donut holes.
2. **Preheat the Air Fryer:** Preheat your air fryer to 350°F (175°C).
3. **Cook the Donuts:** Place the donuts and donut holes in the air fryer basket in a single layer. Depending on the size of your air fryer, you may need to cook in batches. Air fry at 350°F for 5-6 minutes, flipping halfway through, until the donuts are golden brown and cooked through.
4. **Prepare the Cinnamon Sugar:** While the donuts are cooking, mix the granulated sugar and ground cinnamon in a mixing bowl.
5. **Coat the Donuts:** Once the donuts are done, brush them with melted butter while still warm. Immediately toss them in the cinnamon sugar mixture until fully coated.
6. **Serve:** Serve the donuts warm, with the donut holes for an extra treat.
7. **Serve immediately:** Enjoy as a sweet breakfast or snack.

Servings: 8 donuts
Prep time: 10 minutes
Cooking time: 6 minutes

Nutritional info:
Calories: 200
Protein: 2g
Carbs: 24g
Fat: 10g

Quick tips:

- **Biscuit Dough:** You can also use homemade dough if preferred; just adjust cooking time as needed.
- **Extra Crispiness:** For extra crispy donuts, air fry the donut holes for an additional 1-2 minutes.
- **Serving Suggestion:** Pair with a hot cup of coffee or a glass of milk for a perfect start to your day.

Baked Pears with Honey and Walnuts

Air Fryer Baked Pears with Honey and Walnuts are a simple yet elegant dessert that brings out the natural sweetness of ripe pears. Topped with crunchy walnuts and a drizzle of honey, these pears are a healthy and delicious treat that's perfect for any occasion.

Tools needed:

Air fryer
Knife and cutting board
Spoon for scooping

Ingredients:

- 2 ripe pears, halved and cored
- 2 tbsp honey
- 1/4 cup chopped walnuts
- 1/2 tsp ground cinnamon
- 1/4 tsp ground nutmeg (optional)
- Greek yogurt or whipped cream (for serving, optional)

Directions:

1. **Prepare the Pears:** Cut the pears in half lengthwise and use a spoon to scoop out the core and seeds.
2. **Season the Pears:** Sprinkle the pear halves with ground cinnamon and nutmeg (if using). Place them in the air fryer basket, cut side up.
3. **Preheat the Air Fryer:** Preheat your air fryer to 350°F (175°C).
4. **Cook the Pears:** Air fry the pears at 350°F for 10-12 minutes, or until the pears are tender and lightly caramelized.
5. **Add the Toppings:** After cooking, drizzle the pears with honey and sprinkle with chopped walnuts.
6. **Serve:** Transfer the pears to a serving plate and, if desired, serve with a dollop of Greek yogurt or whipped cream.
7. **Serve immediately:** Enjoy as a light dessert or a special breakfast treat.

Servings: 4
Prep time: 5 minutes
Cooking time: 12 minutes

Nutritional info:
Calories: 150
Protein: 2g
Carbs: 25g
Fat: 6g

Quick tips:

- **Pear Variety:** Use firm but ripe pears like Bosc or Anjou for the best texture.
- **Nut Alternatives:** Try using pecans or almonds instead of walnuts for a different flavor.
- **Serving Suggestion:** For an extra touch, drizzle with a little extra honey and sprinkle with some granola.

Air Fryer Apple Crisp

Air Fryer Apple Crisp is a warm, comforting dessert that's quick and easy to make. It features tender, cinnamon-spiced apples topped with a crispy oat and nut crumble. This dessert is perfect for satisfying your sweet tooth with the added convenience of using an air fryer.

Tools needed:

Air fryer
Mixing bowls
Baking dish (oven-safe and air fryer-friendly)
Spoon for mixing

Ingredients:

For the Filling:

- 3 medium apples, peeled, cored, and sliced
- 1 tbsp lemon juice
- 2 tbsp granulated sugar or coconut sugar
- 1 tsp ground cinnamon
- 1/4 tsp ground nutmeg (optional)

For the Crumble Topping:

- 1/2 cup old-fashioned oats
- 1/4 cup almond flour or all-purpose flour
- 1/4 cup chopped nuts (such as walnuts or pecans)
- 2 tbsp melted butter or coconut oil
- 2 tbsp brown sugar or coconut sugar
- 1/2 tsp ground cinnamon
- Pinch of salt

Directions:

1. **Prepare the Apples:** In a mixing bowl, toss the apple slices with lemon juice, sugar, cinnamon, and nutmeg (if using) until evenly coated. Transfer the apples to a greased, air fryer-friendly baking dish.
2. **Make the Crumble Topping:** In another bowl, combine the oats, almond flour, chopped nuts, melted butter, brown sugar, cinnamon, and a pinch of salt. Mix until the ingredients are well combined and the mixture is crumbly.
3. **Top the Apples:** Sprinkle the crumble mixture evenly over the apples in the baking dish.
4. **Preheat the Air Fryer:** Preheat your air fryer to 350°F (175°C).
5. **Cook the Apple Crisp:** Place the baking dish in the air fryer basket. Air fry at 350°F for 15-20 minutes, or until the apples are tender and the topping is golden brown and crispy.
6. **Serve:** Remove the apple crisp from the air fryer and let it cool slightly before serving.
7. **Serve immediately:** Enjoy with a scoop of vanilla ice cream or a dollop of whipped cream for an extra special treat.

Servings: 4 | **Prep time:** 10 minutes | **Cooking time:** 20 minutes

Nutritional info: Calories: 250, Protein: 3g, Carbs: 35g, Fat: 12g

Quick tips:

- **Apple Variety:** Use a mix of tart and sweet apples, like Granny Smith and Honeycrisp, for a balanced flavor.
- **Make Ahead:** Prepare the apple filling and crumble topping separately, then assemble and cook just before serving.
- **Serving Suggestion:** For a richer flavor, add a splash of vanilla extract to the apple filling before baking.

CONCLUSION

As we reach the end of our culinary journey together, I hope you feel inspired and confident in your ability to create delicious, healthy meals with your air fryer. Whether you're a seasoned cook or new to the world of air frying, you've now experienced firsthand how this versatile appliance can transform your kitchen routine. From quick snacks to gourmet dishes, the possibilities are endless, and the results are always satisfying.

As you continue to explore the many uses of your air fryer, remember that cooking is a journey of experimentation and discovery. Don't be afraid to try new recipes, adjust cooking times and temperatures to suit your preferences, and make each dish your own. The quick reference guide provided will be a helpful tool as you become more familiar with your air fryer's capabilities, offering a handy way to ensure your meals turn out perfectly every time.

As you continue to harness the power of your air fryer, remember that cooking is an evolving craft. Each dish you prepare is an opportunity to learn, improve, and delight in the flavors you create. Your air fryer is more than just an appliance—it's a gateway to endless culinary possibilities. Whether you're whipping up a quick weeknight dinner, preparing a special meal for loved ones, or simply experimenting with new ingredients, your air fryer will be there to make the process easier, healthier, and more enjoyable.

Don't hesitate to revisit the recipes we've explored together or to venture into uncharted territory with new ones. The convenience and versatility of the air fryer make it an ideal companion for any cook, from the beginner to the experienced chef. Keep your quick reference guide handy as a go-to resource for cooking times and temperatures, helping you to achieve consistently delicious results.

And remember, the world of air frying is vast and ever-expanding. There are countless communities, blogs, and video tutorials online that can offer new ideas, techniques, and inspiration. Joining these communities not only provides additional support but also connects you with fellow air fryer enthusiasts who share your passion for great food.

For those seeking additional resources and support, there are countless online communities, forums, and recipe collections dedicated to air fryer enthusiasts. Whether you're looking for new recipes, troubleshooting tips, or simply want to share your own culinary creations, these resources can provide a wealth of information and inspiration.

In closing, I encourage you to embrace your air fryer as a trusted ally in the kitchen. With its ability to cook meals quickly and healthily, it's a tool that can truly enhance your cooking experience. So, keep exploring, keep experimenting, and most importantly, keep enjoying the delicious results. Happy cooking!

28-DAY MEAL PLAN

Day	Breakfast	Lunch	Dinner
Day 1	Quinoa Breakfast Bowls with Poached Egg and Avocado	Air Fryer Keto Cauliflower Mac and Cheese	Air Fryer Lamb Kebabs with Cumin and Sumac
Day 2	Air Fryer Chickpea Flour Omelette	Air Fryer Beet Chips with Goat Cheese Dip	Air Fryer Char Siu Pork Belly
Day 3	Miso-Glazed Sweet Potato Toasts with Avocado	Air Fryer Pancetta-Wrapped Scallops	Air Fryer Moroccan Lamb Tagine Skewers
Day 4	Beetroot and Goat Cheese Breakfast Tart	Air Fryer Cauliflower Steaks with Romesco Sauce	Air Fryer Spatchcock Quail with Honey and Thyme
Day 5	Savory Chia Seed Pancakes with Smoked Salmon	Air Fryer Beef Heart Skewers with Chimichurri	Air Fryer Turmeric-Crusted Cod

Day 6	Matcha and Coconut Breakfast Bars	Air Fryer Green Shakshuka	Air Fryer Porchetta with Fennel and Garlic
Day 7	Air Fryer Quiche with Wild Mushrooms and Gruyere	Air Fryer Pancetta-Wrapped Scallops	Coffee-Crusted Pork Tenderloin
Day 8	Zaatar-Spiced Breakfast Flatbreads	Crispy Air Fryer Beef Tongue Tacos	Air Fryer Char Siu Pork Belly
Day 9	Air Fryer Banana Bread Muffins	Stuffed Peppers with Farro, Walnuts, and Feta	Persian-Spiced Chicken Wings with Pomegranate
Day 10	Air Fryer Keto Scotch Eggs	Air Fryer Beet Chips with Goat Cheese Dip	Air Fryer Duck Breast with Pomegranate Glaze
Day 11	Air Fryer Crispy Zucchini Chips	Air Fryer Crispy Tofu with Ginger-Soy Glaze	Air Fryer Blackened Catfish with Remoulade

Day 12	Air Fryer Quiche with Wild Mushrooms and Gruyere	Air Fryer Baked Pears with Honey and Walnuts	Air Fryer Char Siu Pork Belly
Day 13	Miso-Glazed Sweet Potato Toasts with Avocado	Air Fryer Moroccan Lamb Tagine Skewers	Spiced Mackerel with Tamarind and Fennel
Day 14	Air Fryer Beet Chips with Goat Cheese Dip	Air Fryer Pork Satay with Peanut Sauce	Air Fryer Char Siu Pork Belly
Day 15	Matcha and Coconut Breakfast Bars	Air Fryer Chicken Livers with Herb Aioli	Air Fryer Blackened Catfish with Remoulade
Day 16	Zaatar-Spiced Breakfast Flatbreads	Air Fryer Char Siu Pork Belly	Air Fryer Moroccan Lamb Tagine Skewers
Day 17	Air Fryer Pancetta-Wrapped Scallops	Air Fryer Moroccan Lamb Tagine Skewers	Air Fryer Spatchcock Quail with Honey and Thyme

Day 18	Air Fryer Green Shakshuka	Air Fryer Spicy Beef and Kimchi Stuffed Peppers	Air Fryer Char Siu Pork Belly
Day 19	Air Fryer Banana Bread Muffins	Air Fryer Blackened Catfish with Remoulade	Air Fryer Pancetta-Wrapped Scallops
Day 20	Air Fryer Beet Chips with Goat Cheese Dip	Air Fryer Pancetta-Wrapped Scallops	Coffee-Crusted Pork Tenderloin
Day 21	Air Fryer Crispy Zucchini Chips	Air Fryer Beet Chips with Goat Cheese Dip	Air Fryer Char Siu Pork Belly
Day 22	Air Fryer Pancetta-Wrapped Scallops	Air Fryer Moroccan Lamb Tagine Skewers	Air Fryer Spatchcock Quail with Honey and Thyme
Day 23	Air Fryer Banana Bread Muffins	Air Fryer Pancetta-Wrapped Scallops	Air Fryer Char Siu Pork Belly

Day 24	Miso-Glazed Sweet Potato Toasts with Avocado	Air Fryer Spicy Beef and Kimchi Stuffed Peppers	Air Fryer Char Siu Pork Belly
Day 25	Zaatar-Spiced Breakfast Flatbreads	Air Fryer Blackened Catfish with Remoulade	Air Fryer Pancetta-Wrapped Scallops
Day 26	Air Fryer Crispy Zucchini Chips	Air Fryer Moroccan Lamb Tagine Skewers	Coffee-Crusted Pork Tenderloin
Day 27	Air Fryer Pancetta-Wrapped Scallops	Air Fryer Beet Chips with Goat Cheese Dip	Air Fryer Char Siu Pork Belly
Day 28	Air Fryer Green Shakshuka	Air Fryer Pancetta-Wrapped Scallops	Air Fryer Blackened Catfish with Remoulade

RECIPE INDEX

Made in the USA
Las Vegas, NV
29 March 2025

20264425R00057